Making News

Making News

✦

A Straight-Shooting
Guide to Media Relations

David Henderson

iUniverse Star
New York Lincoln Shanghai

Making News
A Straight-Shooting Guide to Media Relations

iUniverse Star
an iUniverse, Inc. imprint

iUniverse books may be ordered through booksellers or by contacting:

iUniverse
2021 Pine Lake Road, Suite 100
Lincoln, NE 68512
www.iuniverse.com
1-800-Authors (1-800-288-4677)

Cover Design by Tina Cardosi, TM Design, Inc.
Author photo by Jerry Errico

ISBN-13: 978-1-58348-468-5 (pbk)
ISBN-13: 978-0-595-82182-2 (ebk)
ISBN-10: 1-58348-468-X (pbk)
ISBN-10: 0-595-82182-0 (ebk)

Printed in the United States of America

To Margo, Mike, Anna and Claire

Contents

Getting to Know the News Media

Rules of Engagement

Media Relations Field Guide

Introduction

I have never thought there was any magic about getting good media coverage for my clients.

An executive at a top public relations agency once told me that media relations — getting your story before the news media — was a science. It is not a science, either.

Effective media relations, the kind that delivers the results you desire, is not magic, and it is not science. It is not even art. It is an imperfect craft, at best. But it can be powerful. Effective media relations comes from knowing what makes a news story, finding a reporter who agrees with you and working with the reporter to develop a story you'll be pleased with. The goal is to reach and influence desired audiences.

This book is about how to make news and control your message through the news media, whether for your organization, your client or yourself. While based on the original idea of my earlier book, "Media Relations," this new work includes an in-depth look at the forces of change within the news business that are also changing how we must approach and work with journalists to get our story reported, today and into the future. The signals are clear that anyone who practices effective media relations must keep pace and embrace new methods. The view is the same but the scenery sure is different.

During media relations workshops and lectures, I have been asked questions about new trends and challenges in working with an ever-changing news media. How good is online technology — such as blogs, streaming video, Web site newsrooms and podcasts? What are just the passing fads, and what's a viable new tool of media relations? What's the future of video news releases? How about the effectiveness of traditional media kits, news conferences and news releases?

"Making News" provides straight-shooting and timely background information, case histories and examples — complete with inside tips, comments and suggestions from working journalists — to give anyone a wider understanding and perspective into how the news business functions, how reporters judge the value of legitimate stories, how to communicate with the media and what reporters need to write your story.

You can achieve significant success when you're smart and fast on your feet, and when you understand the news media's playing field, how to control the message. You can boost brand awareness for an organization, prominently position a product or service, provide clear and accurate information in a crisis, and help to right a wrong, among other desired results. Because of the near-instant credibility and widespread audience reach that comes with news coverage, media relations can be the most influential tool in an organization's marketing strategy.

When I made the career jump from network news correspondent at CBS News to managing partner of a public relations agency, it seemed only natural to me to begin building effective media relations for my clients by figuring out a news angle that would appeal to a particular reporter.

But over the intervening years, I realized few public relations people ever consider what a reporter needs for a story. Even fewer have ever bothered to develop working relationships with the news media, preferring instead to send news releases indiscriminately to as many journalists as possible. And fewer still have any experience actually working in the news business.

In preparing to teach a class on media relations at the University of Virginia, I decided that the approach that made the most sense was to give students an insider's perspective of the news business

- Build a better understanding of what makes a newsperson tick.

- Increase knowledge of what is legitimate news — the kind that's reported each day in newspapers, magazines, online and on television and radio.

- Develop insight into how we can control the direction of a news story that we are involved in, to the best of our ability. That's really the foundation for effective media relations in today's media environment.

I was, however, faced with a dilemma: I wanted a book to share with students but could find nothing, university-level textbook or otherwise, that even had a hint of recognition of the needs of the news media from a journalist's perspective. What I found were traditional how-to books on developing "press materials," as if we really need more *stuff* — most of it unsolicited — flooding the news media. The books I found seemed to be from a bygone era of media relations. Things have changed in a big way.

We are witnessing a seismic transformation of power in the news industry that is — according to the Project for Excellence in Journalism at Columbia University — influenced by the dynamics of technology; audience shifts; changing revenue streams; and always present, never-ending news cycles. I have heard the impact of these changing dynamics expressed over and over by people in the news business as I researched this book. They used those exact words — seismic change — to describe this shift in the news industry, which affects anyone who hopes to get a story in a newspaper or magazine, online, or on the air. Not surprisingly many traditional methods of getting journalists' attention may no longer work.

It's being said within the news industry that the traditional media gatekeepers — publishers, editors and other people who decided what is or is not *news* — no longer have any gates to keep. Perhaps the situation is not quite that stark, but the industry clearly is headed in that direction. The news business is undergoing a major evolution, driven by a massive slump in profits at news organizations, shifts in advertising dollars, changes in consumer interests and new forms of technology such as blogs (weblogs or online journals), podcasts and the Internet. All the emerging online technology is attracting larger and younger audiences, and not many of them are interested in media tradition.

Polls show that younger people, ages 18 to 35, will only occasionally read a newspaper, preferring instead to get their news from online, free sources or Comedy Central's "The Daily Show." Those same polls show declining trust in the news media. In response to these and other signals, the whole news industry is moving to stay vibrant.

To appeal to people who once had the time to read newspapers and sit down to watch network newscasts, we are seeing the emergence of *participatory journalism*. This shift is being called a democratization of the media. The news business and methods for communicating with today's journalist are changing before our eyes. In this book, I will share firsthand insight into this seismic change and how it impacts public and media relations, today and into the future.

For those in public relations, and for anyone else who works with the news media, it is important to track and understand this 21st century evolution of the media, which is likely to continue for years. As the old cliché goes, the only thing constant about the media today is change.

The old, traditional tools of media relations, such as news releases and news conferences, are becoming obsolete. Reporters don't have the time to sort through piles of news releases, preferring instead to rely on trusted sources, relationships and online resources. News conferences have gone the way of the dinosaur. With highly competitive news cycles and downsized newsrooms, many reporters simply don't have the time to cover news conferences anymore.

So this book is a first: a field guide on how to orchestrate effective media relations in today's multimedia world, written from the perspective and based on the experience of working journalists.

My goal in writing this book is to paint an overview of this tide of change in communicating with journalists, share new methods for media relations and explore new trends for getting results today and into the future. Making news — isn't that what it's all about in media relations?

The key to achieving those coveted results — the bottom-line value of media relations that will impress our clients and our bosses — is to watch the signals carefully and to know the inside perspective of some of today's most respected journalists. This will help us understand how we can better practice this imperfect craft of media relations and better represent our clients.

In researching this book, I interviewed the interviewers — more than 100 reporters, editors, producers and news managers — to get their thoughts, insider perspectives and tips. These are journalists at some of the top newspapers, magazines, wire services, online news sites, blogs and broadcast news organizations in America and Britain.

The result is this working guide on making news, written from the viewpoint of journalists. It is a look inside the news business and a resource to help you

- Communicate clearly and accurately with reporters, editors and producers.

- Control messages to target audiences to the best possible extent.

- Craft a story idea to make it sound appealing and easy to cover for a reporter.

- Achieve accurate, credible and effective coverage in the news media.

There are few greater thrills than opening a newspaper or turning on a newscast to see a favorable, balanced news story about your company, your organization or yourself. Accurate news coverage, with its implied third-party endorsement, is credible and considered far more influential than paid advertising.

Effective media relations doesn't work the way that most people think and certainly not the way that many public relations people practice it. It's actually simpler and certainly more straightforward. It's also more powerful than any other component in an organization's marketing arsenal. First and foremost, it is *relationship-based*.

Whether used in building a brand, marketing a product or service, or promoting an image, your knowledge of how the media thinks about news and what they are looking for in a story will give you a significant competitive edge. This tool of knowledge will help you achieve your goal of making news.

Getting to Know the
News Media

Windows of Opportunity

Welcome to life in a multimedia world, an environment that is constantly changing, taking new shape and then reinventing itself all over again. A world in which, for journalists, every minute can be a deadline. A world where what you say in Chicago can be reported almost instantly in London, Singapore and everywhere in between via the Internet, wire services and satellite television news. A world where the diverse and ever-changing dynamics of new information about current events from countless sources are competing for the media's attention. A world where a faceless blogger can write something hostile about your organization and ruin your whole day.

A world where the news media you knew last year isn't the same news media you have to know today.

In today's highly competitive world, a good news story positions you as a leader, as someone special. A news story about your organization isn't just a heady drug for the ego. Having the media write about your organization builds your reputation and enhances your brand. It will help drive awareness and interest in your organization more quickly than anything else. Media coverage opens doors to audiences that might otherwise remain out of reach. Media coverage can make and break legends. A good story in the media can right a wrong.

Yet for many individuals, businesses and organizations aiming to reach wide audiences, effective media relations remains all too elusive. In the last couple of decades, the value of media relations has been recognized as an influential brand-building and marketing tool. Corporations have spent millions on public relations efforts, trying to win favorable positioning in their respective marketplaces by using the awesome reach of the news media, a powerful conduit to the public. Still, many organizations feel shortchanged.

Part of the reason is that not many people who are assigned the task of dealing with journalists or even many so-called media relations experts have ever worked a day in a newsroom. Media relations can be done without such experience, of course, but someone with a background in the working news media generally knows how journalists think; what they are looking for; and what is needed, from the reporter's perspective, to make a *story* — as opposed to so much public relations hype.

When I spoke with Stuart Elliott, who covers the advertising industry for *The New York Times*, he began by saying that calling a reporter with a story should be "a matter of common sense" but what he sees instead on a daily basis is "ignorance."

Ignorance, Elliott said, about what the media needs and how the media works is the biggest fault among public relations people who call him with a story pitch. It's easy, he explained, for a PR person to get a feel for the stories and angles he covers for the *Times* through a quick Google search, but PR people don't seem to bother. Elliott is certainly not alone in this complaint.

Listening to his perspective, which mirrors that of many other newspeople I have interviewed, I couldn't help being struck by the reality that the public relations industry hasn't done a good job, at least in the minds of many newspeople, of keeping up with the times and changing trends in journalism.

Elliott said he is annoyed by continuous calls from media relations people trying to pitch to him something he doesn't cover or to "fix" bad coverage they've gotten someplace else, like a competing newspaper. Most PR people, he said, are neither aware nor sensitive to his story deadlines for the *Times*. All these issues can be easily resolved through training, he said, but he is not seeing any evidence of such improvement. On the contrary, Elliott said he believes it is getting worse.

For decades much of the public relations industry has churned out volumes of press materials in the same old, predictable and dull fashion. They use junior staff members to call and pitch to as many reporters as possible — also usually in a predictable and dull fashion. That's the approach that aggravates Elliott and other respected journalists.

Newspeople are always looking for interesting stories to report. *What reporters ask is that public relations people comprehend the difference between a story and so much PR fluff that wastes their time, and then learn how to present the story idea in a professional and timely manner.*

Then there is the matter of all those news releases that flood into newsrooms around the country each day.

Corporations and not-for-profit organizations alike still spend days working to draft a single news release, often on some self-serving subject, not mindful of whether what they have to say might be of interest to the media or outside audiences.

I've seen executives get so wrapped up in the lengthy process of writing a news release that they lose comprehension of what it is and begin to believe their news release will miraculously capture national headlines. With few exceptions such coverage just doesn't happen. Nonetheless they will draft and rewrite, passing it from executive to attorney and back again. Everyone will initial it. The process can take days. The press release will be filled with glowing quotes about how "thrilled and excited" organization members are about their announcement. And then it's sent out, perhaps on an expensive news-distribution service, to a news media that has seen hundreds of similar news releases that same day, and seldom does anyone in the media really care. The news release that consumed so much time to assemble will just seem to vanish.

Of course the media will get blamed for its bias or for not recognizing the gravitas of the release, but that's not the case at all.

News releases, while a mainstay of traditional media relations, have become one of the least effective methods for focusing the media's attention on something important that you have to say.

Daily newspapers receive thousands of news releases each day. The PR industry has an old habit of overwhelming the media with such releases, most of which never get a second glance in the newsroom.

If you want results in today's media, you need to embrace new approaches and techniques. That's what journalists say. You need to understand the competitive forces of media relations, and you need to be focused and relevant. You need to give reporters a real news story.

In gathering material for this book, I have listened as countless journalists complained that PR people fail to comprehend what makes for a timely and legitimate news story.

Jean Cochran, longtime news anchor on National Public Radio's "Morning Edition," told me, "When someone has asked me how to get their story on NPR, my answer has always been: Make it news. I'm sorry, but the PR business is anathema to me."

Cochran raises a fundamental difference in focus between professional journalists in the mainstream news media and efforts by many PR people to get their clients before the media. Reporters think in terms of legitimate news stories. Yet many PR people often miss the point in understanding that essential fact, she and other journalists say.

"I work in an ivory tower," she says, "where we base our editorial decisions on news values. PR people are in the business of trying to gain free publicity for their clients. And, that's of no use to me as I go about deciding the stories I'm going to write each hour."

Cochran speaks for many journalists who see a need for healthy communications between organizations and the news media yet wish that PR people would better comprehend what the media needs.

Another reporter for a leading weekly news magazine, who asked that I not use his name, was particularly revealing about his feelings toward public relations versus journalism.

"When my DNA split back in college," he said, "and I proceeded down the journalism evolutionary track, I basically stopped thinking about how PR people do their jobs. I'll admit I come across some who seem to merge their interests with mine better than others. But every time I hear a reporter complaining about how clueless a PR person is, I usually say 'Yeah, but imagine what it's like to be the flack for (fill in the CEO name here).' I think about that for about a nanosecond and then it's on to the next story. I have enough work just trying to do my own job well."

The reality is that we live in a highly competitive world filled with smart and busy people fighting for attention to promote a product, a brand or an agenda. It's in that environment that journalists work. Whether they work in broadcast or print, they are trained and paid to find timely and interesting news and to write interesting stories that not only meet their audience's needs and expectations but also help to competitively boost the image of their news organizations.

Jennifer Barrett, an associate editor for *Newsweek*, told me, "I know this may sound dry, but honestly the best pitches are those that come from PR people who have done their homework: they've read my stories, they know my beat and interests, and they've tailored their pitches accordingly.

> "The best pitches are those that come from PR people who have done their homework: they've read my stories, they know my beat and interests, and they've tailored their pitches accordingly." — Jennifer Barrett, associate editor, *Newsweek*

"I have established rapport with a few publicists I really trust. And when they pitch me a story, I immediately take notice. I am more skeptical of new names.

"And, it really peeves me," Barrett said, "when publicists with whom I don't have a working relationship use slang or the type of language that my friends would use in personal e-mails — like emoticons (☺) and 'What's up?' — or when a PR person I don't know (and who has not explained to me who his or her clients are) asks, 'What are you working on?' I know that sounds kind of harsh, but rather than ask that question, it would be helpful if PR people just sent me a list of their clients and a list of topics on which they could comment."

Barrett's message is clear: She prefers to work with trusted sources and media relations people who demonstrate a high level of professional skill and competence. She seeks only legitimate stories ... and those that don't waste her time with trivia.

While researching this book, I've heard Barrett's sentiments again and again as I have talked with journalists. Her perspective is echoed by Lisa Mullins, the anchor and senior producer of "The World," an international news program produced by BBC News and heard on public radio stations across America. "It usually takes a nanosecond to determine whether a publicist knows our program, anticipates what sparks our interest, and even believes in what he or she is pitching," Mullins said. "All of these things affect a PR person's credibility. And once that credibility is gone, it's hard to get it back. Honesty is hugely important. I want to be able to trust your pitch."

Marcus Chan, a technology editor at the *San Francisco Chronicle*, told me that he is "amazed" at how often PR people don't do their basic homework.

"I'm often pitched on topics or products," he said, "that — had the PR person researched our coverage — would know that they were of little interest to us. I'm also amazed by PR folks who leave me voice mails asking which reporter covers a particular industry."

Sometimes — in fact more often than not — a story needs an unusual twist to cut through competitive clutter and get the media's attention. My colleagues in the public relations industry might call it *spin*, but that word has lost some credibility in recent years, as too often spin is associated with trying to make a topic legitimate when it's not. When you employ an unusual twist, on the other hand, you are using your imagination to come up with a clever new way to present a real, honest-to-goodness story to the media.

Let me share an example. In a tough competitive bid against a major entertainment publicity firm in Los Angeles, my agency won the account to launch the new image of a still relatively unknown community called Branson, Missouri. Branson is a place where many respected senior citizen stars of the country music world have settled and continue to perform.

Andy Williams has his Moon River Theater there. The Presley family (no relation to the King of Rock 'n' Roll) has their Country Jubilee Theater. Ray Stevens has his own theater, and so does a popular country music violinist named Shoji Tabuchi. More than 30 luxurious music halls have been built in Branson in the last 15 years.

No one seems to know why this started or why so many country music performers were attracted to Branson, but the theaters are filled with fans every afternoon and evening, and the shows are terrific. Perhaps Branson is best chalked up as a middle-class American phenomenon.

When my strategic communications agency began working with Branson, awareness of the town was limited to a few surrounding states. Attendance at its shows was an already fairly impressive 1.3 million a year. But local entertainment leaders had a bigger dream.

Theater owners had formed an association, the Ozark Marketing Council, which was our client. They had two goals: achieve national awareness for Branson and push up the annual number of visitors to 3.5 million within two years. They wanted to meet those goals solely through media relations.

Clearly an entertainment publicity angle focusing on the individual country music stars could not meet those goals. That approach, while fairly logical, just could not reach and excite the sheer number of people that Branson needed, because the approach would be limited largely to the entertainment media.

Our plan was to capitalize on Branson's allure of being relatively unknown — something new and trendy. A little research showed that Branson had already eclipsed Nashville in annual visitors and was starting to get into the league of places like Disney World. So we planned a "grand opening" of Branson's new season of stars, and the pitch to the national news media went something like this:

"Let me tell you about a place you have never heard of. It's called Branson, Missouri. It's in the Ozarks of southern Missouri and only reachable by two-lane mountain blacktop. But last year Branson attracted nearly one-third the total number of tourists of Disney World. And yet you have never heard of the place. Right?" We always stopped there to let those impressive nuggets of information sink in and get a reaction.

Then we continued, "The tourists are there because nearly every country music star you can name — from Andy Williams to the Gatlin Brothers to Mel Tillis — is performing at the dozens of music halls along that two-lane blacktop. And the biggest season ever starts in three weeks. Everybody will be there ..." By the end of that pitch, we usually had their attention.

Many news decision makers would ask us who else was covering the story. It was a legitimate question, considering the timely nature of our pitch and the competitiveness of the media. At first, when we had no firm commitments, we would answer, "Well, we are getting a lot of interest from so-and-so," and drop the names of their competitors. It was a true claim, because most of the newspeople we contacted expressed real interest.

We straightforwardly communicated that Branson was expected to be a big story that season, and there would be competition for the story. Within the world of the news business, that translates into "if we're not there, we'll get scooped by our competitors!"

Then what can only be described as a snowball effect happened. One major news organization confirmed they would come, then another, and another. Soon the momentum was almost beyond our comprehension. I recall calling our client to say that the "CBS Morning Show" wanted to originate live for nearly a week from the Ray Stevens Theater. An hour later, we confirmed the "The Larry King Show."

When The Associated Press ran an advance national story for us about all the excitement building for the upcoming opening of Branson's biggest season ever, things really heated up. Then *TIME* ran a cover story on Branson, and our phones rang constantly with other news organizations wanting to know how to be a part of the action.

For the people who ran Branson, a different kind of snowball was forming. They were getting calls from other country music stars who wanted to join in. Soon people like Willie Nelson, Johnny Cash, Glen Campbell and Loretta Lynn were showing up to perform at the town's music halls.

In retrospect I would describe the event as country music's version of Woodstock, except that in Branson the fans were entertained by a fellow dressed as a hobo named Steamboat Willie, among others, while at Woodstock they heard Richie Havens, Jimi Hendrix and the performers of another genre.

By the time the season opened, the narrow roads of Branson were filled not only with country music enthusiasts but also with satellite trucks from television networks and stations across the country.

During that two-week grand opening at Branson, we attracted coverage and live broadcasts by "The Today Show," "CBS Morning News," *TIME, People, Newsweek,* "NBC Evening News," "CBS Evening News," "ABC Evening News," The Associated Press, Reuters, *The New York Times,* "The Larry King Show," countless local television news remotes from across the country, too many newspapers to count and, of all things, *The Wall Street Journal,* which wrote a glowing editorial about the Branson phenomenon.

One day during the high point of the coverage, we got all the country music stars together for a photo event on a large hilltop meadow in Branson. There were more cameras than at a White House news conference, sending images across the country.

Literally overnight millions of people all across America learned about Branson, and all because of media relations.

Incidentally we never sent out a single news release. Not one. Rather we did our homework to identify the correct reporters and editors — journalists who have covered similar faddish and slightly out-of-the-ordinary events before — and then got on the telephones to pitch them with an appealing story.

Branson's star took off like, well, a shooting star. That season alone, the town attracted more than 3 million visitors. There were traffic jams for days on that now-famous two-lane blacktop. The theaters, theme parks, motels, curio shops and restaurants were packed — and it hasn't let up since. Branson, Missouri, became a world-famous entertainment mecca almost overnight, and it all began with a clever twist on a timely and trendy story for the news media.

Our approach in presenting the story to the media had focused not on the obvious — the dozens of country music stars performing at Branson — but on a phenomenon that appealed to the national news media. Here was an entertainment center that few decision makers at the major media centers were aware of but was attracting millions of visitors.

Our strategy was to play to the natural curiosity of the newspeople who decide what is reported. Most of them are in New York and, at the time, most of those folks in New York had never heard of Branson. The phenomenon captured their curiosity.

One of the easiest ways to achieve good media relations seems to be the hardest for public relations people to understand. People in the news business make their living writing stories that appear in newspapers, wire services, and magazines, and on television and radio. To do this they need something new or different — a hook, an angle. Learn what they need for a news angle, give them a legitimate story, provide balanced background information, and the news media will be happy. And you will have a good story to your credit.

Journalism Driven by Profits and Fear

To understand effective media relations is to understand the news business and where it's headed. The way in which the business called journalism is practiced by news organizations today has changed at almost the speed of light in recent years. Journalism once focused on reporting events of interest and happenings that might affect our lives. Now, the prime goal of news is maximizing profits.

The mainstream news media is embattled. Attacked by political and societal forces both right and left, rocked by scandals, and challenged by upstart bloggers and the changing landscape of technology, the media has become a focus of controversy and concern. Audiences are in decline, and the media's credibility with the public is in shreds. It hasn't always been this way, but there is general agreement that the media's reputation began to deteriorate when conglomerates got into the news business and were interested solely in the bottom line.

These changes in the business of journalism today have a direct impact on the practice of media relations and our efforts to work with reporters to generate news stories and coverage.

Newsroom staff cutbacks have rocked many news organizations. The venerable *Washington Post* is no exception and a typical example. The paper's number of paid subscribers has declined at a rate of 4 percent a year. During a March 2006 meeting in the *Post*'s newsroom to explain why 80 newspeople would be laid off, Executive Editor Leonard Downie told them, "It is obvious that a significant change is taking place in our readership, with a sizable portion of it migrating to the Internet."

In the Philadelphia metropolitan area, the number of newspaper reporters has fallen from 500 to 220 in the last 20 years, according to the Project for Excellence in Journalism at Columbia University. A few years back, five AM radio stations covered news around the city; now there are two. The project describes it as a "seismic transformation" on the media landscape. It is the trend in the media today across America, but it wasn't always that way.

When I walked into the main newsroom of CBS Network News in New York some years ago as a very naive young man from northern Virginia to begin my career as a television journalist, it was a legendary place. I worked alongside some of the icons of broadcast news: Walter Cronkite, Douglas Edwards, Richard C. Hottelet, Dan Rather, Mike Wallace, Dallas Townsend, Morley Safer. I had always wanted to be a broadcast journalist, and here I was, among some of the best and working for an organization that defined broadcast news excellence. It was one of the most exciting times in my life.

No one back then thought of CBS News as a profit center. It had gotten the moniker "the Tiffany network" because of its focus on quality, in both programming and news. CBS set the example for others to follow. The purpose of CBS News and the other networks was to credibly report the news of the day without being encumbered by an eye on ratings and corporate stock value.

At that time CBS News had a full staff of seasoned editors and producers who checked the facts and looked over every script before it went on the air. So it was at many of the major networks and papers: We would try to find the facts and write stories as accurately and objectively as humanly possible. The emphasis was on quality and solid journalism. We were expected to report the news. Television news in those days made a profound impact on America. It's not that way today.

TV news today is formula-based, entertainment-driven and designed to make money. The more sensational the story or the greater the threat of fear it generates, the larger the potential audience and the higher the advertising rates the news organization can extract.

Especially since Sept. 11, fear sells. That explains the unending emphasis on "Fox News Alerts" in bold red letters on our television screens and similar tactics at other TV news outlets.

"Our history will be what we make it. And if there are any historians about fifty or a hundred years from now, and there should be preserved the kinescopes for one week of all three networks, they will there find recorded in black and white, or in color, evidence of decadence, escapism, and insulation from the realities of the world in which we live."

Sounds like a fairly accurate description of television news today, doesn't it? Edward R. Murrow, the legendary CBS newscaster, spoke those words in October 1958.

> "Our history will be what we make it. And if there are any historians about fifty or a hundred years from now, and there should be preserved the kinescopes for one week of all three networks, they will there find recorded in black and white, or in color, evidence of decadence, escapism, and insulation from the realities of the world in which we live." — Edward R. Murrow

"Evidence of decadence, escapism, and insulation from the realities of the world ..." I guess television news hasn't come too far. In fact journalists from every corner of the news industry have expressed concern to me over whether the journalism profession has lost its compass and is going in a circle rather than improving and moving forward.

Murrow went on to say, "I am frightened by the imbalance, the constant striving to reach the largest possible audience for everything; by the absence of a sustained study of the state of the nation."

Over the last 20 years, many once-respected news operations have dramatically cut back on news staffs, and quality has suffered.

About the state of television news today, CBS newsman Dan Rather told an audience at Fordham University in the summer of 2005 that there is a climate of fear running through newsrooms stronger than he has ever seen in his more than four-decade career. Politicians of "every persuasion," he said, "have gotten better at applying pressure on the conglomerates that own the broadcast networks" in their attempt to influence news.

Rather called it a "new journalism order," and he believes that with the advent of the 24-hour cable news competition, it has led to "dumbed-down, tarted-up" coverage in a desperate chase for ratings. "All of this creates a bigger atmosphere of fear in newsrooms," Rather said. Reporters are cautious, Rather suggested, about covering stories that might be too controversial or might offend an influential group and, consequently, jeopardize the journalist's livelihood.

Aaron Brown, the former CNN anchorman, contended that "truth no longer matters" in the push by 24-hour cable television news channels to build audience ratings. America has become such a polarized society of the left and the right, he said, that many people are not interested in the truth as much as news that conforms to their viewpoints and entertains them.

Once an altruistic and perhaps too idealistic profession with keen focus on balance, accuracy and integrity, journalism is today driven by corporate profits ... money. Big media conglomerates discovered in the 1980s that news, like entertainment, could be a money machine. The higher their ratings in radio and television news, the more they could demand from advertisers. The bigger the headlines in print, the bigger the flow of ad dollars.

Consequently news today is presented less to inform and more to titillate, seduce and entertain. All this has happened at a time when news audiences are being pulled away from traditional news outlets by cable television and Internet news sources.

Television news, for example, has become not so much about providing depth of understanding for a story but about entertainment and drama. Television reporters are also expected to be actors. They are coached on how to lean into the camera while on the air in an attempt to better engage viewers and to use their hands, fingers outstretched, to somehow suggest more meaning and passion to their words in much the same style of those people selling used cars, cleaning supplies and discount furniture on TV commercials. I saw one TV reporter who was so animated and dramatic that he reminded me of one of those ubiquitous salesmen of discount furniture and appliances on late-night TV. So much for journalism's time-honored tradition of dispassionate reporting.

Television news coaches today tell reporters and anchorpeople where and how to stand in order to convey more meaning in their on-air appearances. One trainer told me that he wants to see reporters stand in front of an open door or window, when possible, to suggest depth in what they are saying on the air. I listened patiently, resisting the urge to suggest that he was out of his mind.

Today's TV reporters are coached and rehearsed on ways to use their voice to communicate real care and sincerity for what they are saying even though their words might not. It's not unlike what a film or stage actor does to rehearse for a theatrical part, except TV newspeople are reporting news of the day. They are intentionally putting editorial spin on news stories with voice inflection.

It's a method of sounding sympathetic or exuberant to create some level of drama by emphasizing the wrong words and ending thoughts or sentences with your voice going up in pitch, rather than the customary drop. I bet you would think twice about inviting someone into your living room who came to the front door and spoke in such a contrived, pretentious manner. If you do invite them in, better hide the silver.

Normal people don't communicate that way with one another, and it sounds odd on the air even though it's become an accepted style. To me, this new style of speaking in television news, copied by many reporters and newsreaders, reminds me of those nursery-rhyme recordings my children listened to years ago that featured the voice of a woman who seemed to be talking down to my children in a simple and patronizing manner.

I am often asked during media relations workshops why it is that local TV news reporters can't get their facts correct when they report stories given to them by public relations professionals. It's not surprising; inaccuracy has become a signature of local TV newscasts. Pitching stories to local TV news reporters is always a roll of the dice … and more often than not, you'll lose.

The reality is that many local TV reporters, always with an eye on maybe making it big-time on a network or cable channel, are more consumed with concocting stories that convey shock, fear and gore — the standard formula of local television news today — and with career enhancement than with delivering well-balanced stories.

News departments quietly pay consultants for story angles designed to hype newscast audience numbers, especially during rating periods — the infamous sweeps, when audience viewing habits are sampled to measure the competitive forces within each television market. Capturing the coveted No. 1 spot allows a station to charge the highest amount for commercials.

Here's a real example: A local television news team in Washington, D.C., singled out a real estate company at random for a concocted "investigative" story about possible fair-housing violations during a ratings sweeps period. There was nothing investigative about the story. In fact there wasn't even a story, because there had been no complaints and the company had done nothing wrong.

The reporter got the idea, not from a local tip about something possibly being awry, but from an out-of-town TV news consultant who suggested the story to hype ratings. The story angle had been decided before the reporter and cameraperson even left the TV station.

What appeared on the air was out of context, full of innuendo and inaccurate. The story was merely intended to boost ratings. It suggested there was a fair-housing problem in the community when none existed. Yet it managed to alarm local officials and civic leaders, and it smeared the real estate company's image. This sort of reporting by local television happens every day in cities across America.

My advice is always to first take your stories to either a newspaper or wire service first, where a higher level of journalistic integrity still exists. In fact one of the best ways to get your story on local television news in the most accurate manner possible is to first get the story in print. Television news decision makers — network, local and cable — have traditionally felt more comfortable running a story that first appeared in print.

A producer for ABC News told me that the fierce competitiveness of her industry breeds insecurity in the TV news business. Newscast producers want to feel safe when they make decisions on which story will make it on the air, she said. So they are more comfortable running stories that first appeared in the newspaper. She said a print story seems to "validate" the importance of the story for TV.

For as long as anyone can remember, it has often been the habit of television news to follow or react to major stories that first appeared in newspapers. A big story appears on the front page of the morning paper, and throughout the day and into the evening, it's recycled by television news, often with little new information.

This means that the news industry, operating in a fiercely competitive arena, has lost both the interest and pulse of its audiences and is searching frantically for ways to attract them back. Audiences have too many choices these days to find out what's happening in the world … or be entertained.

Former CNN Anchorman Aaron Brown said, "Television is the most perfect democracy. You sit there with your remote control and vote." This is good for audiences yet bad for news organizations and clearly a challenge in trying to do media relations when it comes to achieving the results we and our clients desire.

"We're in a period of change and dislocation," said Tom Rosenstiel of Columbia University's Graduate School of Journalism. "Clearly, some of the older media are suffering."

Trust in news sources is down drastically, according to a study called "The State of the News Media 2004" by the Project for Excellence in

Journalism, a project Rosenstiel headed at Columbia University, funded by the Pew Charitable Trusts.

According to the Columbia study, the percentage of people who believe what they read in newspapers declined from 80 percent in 1985 to 59 percent in 2003, and the percentage who give high grades for credibility to the network news divisions dropped from 74 percent in 1996 to 65 percent in 2002.

In television the study found a declining amount of airtime devoted to actual news, as opposed to other content, like commercials and promotions. Taken together, the nightly network newscasts, which run for 30 minutes, average 18 minutes and 48 seconds of news, down 11 percent from 1991. On network morning shows, the average is 15 minutes and six seconds of news per half hour.

The study found that English-language newspaper circulation has declined 11 percent since 1990, while network evening newscast ratings are down 34 percent over the last decade.

In general, the study found, corporate profits have increased or held steady while investments in newsgathering have declined. Today, newspapers employ 2,200 fewer people than they did in 1990. Between 1991 and 2000, newspaper profits increased 207 percent, the study found, but newsroom jobs increased just 3 percent.

Overall we have seen significant, almost shocking, waves of layoffs at daily newspapers in recent years. We're not buying newspapers the way we once did, and cherished advertising budgets are not what they once were, diluted even more today by cable, the Internet and other forms of communication with large audiences.

"With department stores consolidating both their operations and their advertising and with readers canceling the newspapers that land on their doorstep in favor of more instant gratification of the Web," David Carr wrote in *The New York Times*, "big newspapers full of deep reporting and serious ambitions seem like dinosaurs at the beginning of a very cold age."

A similar trend is clear in television. The number of correspondents employed by the evening newscasts is down more than 33 percent since 1985, and the number of overseas bureaus has been cut to less than half.

In cable news, again according to the Columbia study, 62 percent of the airtime consists of live broadcasts, which are often cheaper than prepared, packaged reports. And the vast majority of stories reported on cable consist of a few "big stories" of the day.

In one 16-hour broadcast day, the study shows, only 27 percent of stories were new reports that hadn't been mentioned earlier. Fully 68 percent of stories were segments that repeated the same information over and over again, without any new reporting.

The result, the study said, is "jumbled, chaotic, partial quality in some reports, without much synthesis ... of the information." As the satirist Jon Stewart has observed, much of television news has turned into a "nonsensical gong show."

Respected television journalists who are put in the position of working in today's entertainment news environment often jump back in shock.

The highly acclaimed public affairs channel C-SPAN and the cable news giant CNN once teamed up temporarily in a cooperative venture that seemed to have benefits for both parties — greater public awareness for C-SPAN and greater respectability for CNN. It meant that C-SPAN hosts would work stints as news anchors on CNN. The arrangement didn't last long.

C-SPAN chief operating officer and program host Susan Swain told me that when she briefly took up on-air duties at CNN, there was little time to focus on the stories as a responsible journalist. The frantic production pace, the distractions of reading to the precise timing of promotional music and CNN's various computer-generated sound effects — intended to build anticipation for upcoming stories — overshadowed clarity in reporting news. It was all about generating excitement and drama, she observed. It was show business.

It's no different at the other cable and satellite news channels. The once-respected lines between news, shameless promotion, contrived and staged reality shows, and commercials are today no more than a blur, making it difficult for a viewer to discern between hype for the news story, hype for an advertiser or hype for entertainment programming. Communicating the news of the day in a clear and accurate manner takes a backseat.

With the exception of the "NewsHour with Jim Lehrer" on PBS, many news stories on television networks, local stations and cable channels are intentionally designed to be more dramatic through the use of sound effects and music that might fit the mood of stories, according to news producers. Among all the swoosh and swish noises that augment the drama of today's TV newscasts, a reporter friend called my attention to one sound effect on the cable news channel MSNBC that seemed very similar to that of a toilet flushing. He was right. Whether that sound speaks for the state of television news today is another matter.

Newscast producers today make an auditory editorial impact using the same sound effects used in the production of action-packed major motion pictures. It all began with a video editing device called Avid that allowed producers of motion pictures to enhance the visual impact of a scene with unusual, dramatic and seemingly unreal sound effects. If you've been to an action movie in recent years, you no doubt have experienced the floor-shaking sonic booms and heightened sound effects. Chances are that came from an Avid or a similar special-effects device.

From major motion pictures, the sound effects moved to television sports to boost the impact, and then into regular television programs and eventually to newscasts, adding to today's blur between entertainment and news on television. What's real, and what's not? Only the sound-effects editor knows. Here's the dilemma: Special effects in a motion picture can be cool and exciting. Using sound effects to bring drama to television news is editorializing and manipulating the effect of the news.

I remember walking through old town Alexandria, Virginia, near my home, the morning after Hurricane Isabel struck in 2003 to see how much of the town was flooded. I stood at the intersection of King and Fairfax streets along with friends and neighbors to witness the floodwaters that had encroached to a surprising level in our town. The television news satellite trucks were there too, and their reporters were live on the air, waving their hands around in that dramatic fashion that's so popular today.

That evening, watching reports about the flooding on local TV with a friend, we were struck by the use of funereal music in the news report, as if to underscore the gravity of the situation. My friend remarked sardonically that she hadn't heard any music when we stood in the middle of King Street, watching floodwaters creep into stores and homes. Such gimmicks, commonplace in television news today, work to manipulate ordinary stories into editorial statements with entertainment and theatrical overtones.

Ethical conduct on television news programs has come a long way from the meticulous set of policies developed by Richard Salant, the popular president of the CBS News division in the 1970s who wanted the credibility of news separated from sports and other entertainment projects. His directives prohibited music and sound effects from any news program. Sadly those days are gone.

Today's news business is increasingly opinionated and salacious, with the driving forces of news leaders locked in competitive struggles. The only constant about the news media today is change, as one reporter remarked.

It is in this environment that today's media relations professional works. If you are getting the impression that we've got to be fast on our feet to get our story before a moving target, you're right. It's more challenging and more competitive than ever before to get the media's attention and achieve accurate, responsible and meaningful coverage.

The task requires a savvy understanding of news media trends and relationship-building methods to get to know journalists.

While it used to be that all we needed to do was give a reporter a good idea for a story and they'd run with it, today we must be prepared to provide a lot more, including anything that will help a reporter convince his or her editor that the story is worthwhile and relevant.

The discipline of professional media relations today requires that we nurture the story-development process even after we've found interest from a journalist.

We must be prepared to provide all kinds of background information, details and guidance to a reporter, while always keeping the focus on how we would like the story to come out. More often than not, we need to do the legwork for a newsperson in order for it to happen — something unheard of just a few years ago. It's often time-consuming, but necessary, and the payoff is big when you land great coverage.

Here's a tip: If you want to control the news angle of a story you are taking to the media, write it first. Draft a story of about 300 to 400 words in length and really work to make it read like a legitimate story, exactly like something you might want to read in tomorrow's newspaper. Then, when you pitch the story to a reporter, you will have a better focus of how the story elements — the interviews, facts, background information, other viewpoints — should come together for the reporter you have approached. Heck, you might even give the draft to the reporter under the guise of "background materials." I bet you will find that parts of your own version just may appear in the reporter's final story.

Is media relations worth all the effort? You bet! The news media, despite its sometimes rocky and profit-driven evolution over the last couple of decades, remains the most powerful form of communication in America — second only to a couple of people swapping gossip over the office water cooler. So let's get in the ring and work to make news.

It's All About Who You Know

Journalists don't give most people in public relations, with a few exceptions, high marks for knowing how to develop a legitimate news story, getting the story before the news media and cultivating trusted relationships with reporters and editors.

Reporters want trusted sources for stories, and most I have interviewed are open to relationships with public relations people who can be a source of news for their beat or coverage area. The fact is that these relationships are critical to getting the results you expect in media relations.

Judy Feldman at *Money* magazine was succinct when she told me, "It's always great to be able to call someone who you know and ask, 'What's up?'"

For many public relations agencies, however, media relations efforts have remained stalled for too long, bogged down by predictability and traditional tactics, and simply not keeping pace. These efforts often come up short in the areas of authentic, trusted media relationships, journalistic skills and the knowledge of what makes news.

And all too often the key assignment of pitching stories to the news media is handed to the youngest members of a public relations agency who may have little or no training or preparation.

So many PR firms suffer from a counterproductive dichotomy: Their clients expect the professionals to have the media contacts and skills. Yet too many agency executives consider pitching reporters to be beneath them, and the execs hand off the assignment to junior employees and interns with little or no training to actually do the work, sink or swim.

"Sometimes they sound as bored and rote as a telemarketer, and you know the PR agency has dispensed an intern to read off a sheet," said Linda Stasi, a columnist at the *New York Post*. "Don't waste my precious daily deadline time like this. It's not fair to me, and it's not fair to the poor intern who probably gets the brunt of it all!"

On one hand media relations at most agencies is bread and butter, yet on the other hand the work is treated as a ... well, as a bother, as if the agency employees had better things to do. The message is clear that many agencies have gotten lazy about the changing styles of media relations. Therein is a big opportunity for anyone who wants to do a better job.

In response to client concerns, improving media relations skills has been targeted as a top priority by several major public relations agencies in the United States and Britain. Clients have an ever-increasing need to reach audiences through the media in a timely way. Unquestionably corporate clients of PR firms, constantly seeking a competitive edge, want strategic counsel and lofty ideas. But they also want the immediate payoff of effective media relations.

Clients expect public relations experts to have deep media connections and close working relationships with all the most powerful journalists, whether in times of crisis or for routine product promotion. That is just not the case at so many agencies.

"Media relations," said Brian Lamb, founder and chief executive officer of C-SPAN, "is about relationships. A reporter needs to know who you are. It's as important as what you have to say. If you have a great announcement but have not established a contact or relationship in the media, no one will pay attention."

> "Media relations is about relationships. A reporter needs to know who you are. It's as important as what you have to say. If you have a great announcement but have not established a contact or relationship in the media, no one will pay attention." — Brian Lamb, founder and chief executive officer, C-SPAN

Lamb's words get incisively to the core of effective media relations today. It's all about establishing relationships with journalists. But it's hard for PR people to develop those relationships if they don't understand how people in the media operate.

Public relations people "are not sensitive enough to deadlines," said National Public Radio's Barbara Bradley Hagerty of the public relations people who contact her. "They don't bother to ask, to find out whether you are in the middle of something, they just launch into a pitch. Most public relations people don't know how journalists work. Most PR people are not quick enough in responding."

Michele Chandler, a technology reporter for *The Mercury News* in San Jose, told me that she would primarily encourage PR representatives to make sure they are sending pitches to the proper people. "I routinely receive e-mails and phone pitches for healthcare-related stories, a beat I have not had in two years," she said.

Her message is clear: Meaningful results from your efforts in media relations happen when you get to know the right people in the media.

Chandler recommends that people "query first by e-mail, unless you absolutely, positively know the reporter and what beat they cover. When doing a follow-up call, be prepared to back up why the particular event or person or company you're pitching is newsworthy or whether what's being highlighted is part of a wider trend."

In other words, she, like all other journalists, is looking for timely news with a purpose. If your story signals the leading edge of a trend, all the better.

Richard Danbury, producer for "Newsnight" on BBC Television News in London, said, "Many public relations people (not all) are quite unsophisticated. Then again, I suppose many journalists are unsophisticated, too."

Danbury faulted PR people for arrogance in their lack of sophistication, as he called it, and being too lazy to research the media before pitching a story.

"I'm not impressed with the job PR people do," said Pat Piper, longtime broadcast producer and writer for Larry King. "If I say 'no thanks' — I get a bunch of crap about why I'm wrong and how the boss will be contacted."

There's frustration not far below the surface when journalists share their difficulties in dealing with PR people. If a story goes wrong, what most often happens is the impulse to heap blame on the reporter, when the reality of the situation is that the story might not have been accurately pitched or communicated to the news media in the first place. Journalists also feel bombarded with pitches that are completely irrelevant to what they do.

NPR's Jean Cochran has a pet peeve with all the people trying to pitch her with stories that they think would be "perfect" for NPR. She gets literally hundreds of e-mails each week, she said, from people who want stories about their cause or product on the popular news and information radio network.

"I'm not the person to approach," she told me. "Please explain to readers of your book, David, that I only focus on the latest news of the day for my newscasts. It's a tight schedule to do seven newscasts each day. People with hopes of getting their feature stories on the air somehow get the idea that because they hear me read the newscasts, I might be interested in their stories for all of NPR. They need to learn that I am the wrong person to pitch with their feature ideas. I don't have time to track down their feature stories, and their e-mails only clog my inbox."

The problem is usually simple: Public relations people just have not invested the time to know how the news media works, what the journalists need for a story idea, who to contact in the media or how to make a story pitch.

A group of University of Delaware Cooperative Extension educators and scientists, not PR people, decided to take matters into their own hands to find new ways to improve relations with the news media in their state.

Their goal was to see more of their stories in the local media, and the way they handled the project was impressive by any measure. Their first step was to ask a group of journalists to meet with them, face-to-face, and give them the straight story about how the media works. I was lucky enough to attend as a guest.

The session took place at Rehoboth, Delaware, a location that was remote enough to be a couple of hours' drive for most people, including the reporters. The session revealed the professional commitments of all involved to enhance the reputation of their news organizations and trade.

Watching the interchange, I was struck by the realization of how seldom public relations agencies and many corporation communications departments of organizations meet in such a forum to learn new trends and techniques and to build relationships. Yet a group of University of Delaware educators and scientists had figured out how to get better coverage.

The journalists represented the spectrum of the news media in Delaware and included Luladey Tadesse, a business reporter for *The News Journal* in Wilmington, Delaware; Jenni Pastusak, a reporter and anchor at WBOC television news in Salisbury, Maryland; and Dennis Forney, publisher of the *Cape Gazette* in Lewes, Delaware.

Pastusak explained the need for local television news to come up with stories that appeal primarily to women, age 25 to 35. That's her audience, and the target of the station's advertising. At her TV station, stories are aimed at an imaginary viewer named "Lisa" who wants to know about threats to her family, such as a new flu outbreak; who will stop what she is doing to watch stories about health issues and well-being; and, who will be touched by news features with "hard-hitting" emotional appeal. Pastusak underscored the importance of news sources, saying that she calls people she knows in the community to get stories for her newscasts.

The signal was clear that local television news in "the world of Lisa," as Pastusak described it, might not appeal to all of us, but it's where local television is today. It might not be the depth of reporting we would like to see, but in America, it is formula-driven local TV that brings in advertising dollars.

Tadesse, who originally worked at the *Los Angeles Times* before coming to Delaware, spoke of building her network of news contacts throughout the state with ordinary people she had met while doing business stories — people who became trusted resources for other stories. Again, it's all about relationships.

Dennis Forney was the old-timer in the group. He's been a respected newspaperman in Delaware for over three decades. His definition of news is simple: Give him a timely story he hasn't heard before, and put a human face on it. Don't send him a news release; just pick up the phone and give him a call. News releases don't result in news stories. And personal contact with the news media helps you cut through competitive clutter and be noticed.

The common message that these journalists shared with the University of Delaware group was that reporters today rely on solid, trusted contacts and sources — relationships, in other words — to develop stories. Relationships. It's all about who you know in a newsroom and what they need for a story.

"PR people just don't do their homework," said Steve Scully, long-time producer at C-SPAN. "For example, don't call me about a segment on gardening, when C-SPAN does politics, issues, books and events."

Then there are those journalists you cannot approach with a story pitch. This group includes many editorial writers, columnists and many broadcast anchorpeople. It's hit or miss, of course, but usually comes down to your personal relationship as a credible news source to the newsperson.

Frank Rich at *The New York Times* shared with me, "My column is self-generated, and when I deal with PR people, it's at my instigation, not theirs, usually because I want specific information." As he said that,

I thought ... *and the PR people Frank Rich is likely to call are people he knows and trusts.* Yes, it's all about relationships and who you know.

During my research for this book, a well-known editorial writer at *The New York Times* politely declined my request to discuss media relations, because he does not want to reveal his newsgathering and writing style. I completely respect his position. Nonetheless he is one of the most open and accessible editorial writers on the planet, and in a quiet, subtle manner, he disclosed something about his style: He is reachable, he is open. You can contact him. It's not done through an expensive, customized news release service but rather on the direct personal level of simply sending him an e-mail. He had responded to me within an hour.

Media relations nonetheless remains a mystery for many executives and PR practitioners — a seemingly vague thing that often involves hiring an agency to do something intangible, that may or may not have any results. It is common to hear company executives express their displeasure to their public relations people at having spent vast sums of money on media relations campaigns that totally miss the mark.

Many journalists are fully aware that corporations often fumble and miss excellent opportunities to be heard and gain valuable publicity when their public relations people don't have the right connections and knowledge of the media.

Andrew Buncombe, Washington correspondent for London's *The Independent* newspaper, said, "Sometimes I cannot believe the opportunities that big companies let pass when I am seeking a comment from them on a story that is at worst neutral and at best very much in their favor. Some [public relations people] are pathetic."

The most important thing, Buncombe said, "is to understand the market and understand the media outlet you are trying to pitch the story to. No media organization operates without a degree of bias in the stories they promote. The PR person needs to study that."

There many stories, however, of how media-aware public relations professionals have helped big companies capture the moment.

Here's one: During the megamerger of the railroad giants Conrail and CSX Transportation, the team at Edelman Public Relations that was working on behalf of CSX became keenly aware that safety was the top issue. The Federal Railroad Administration (FRA) had said that its primary concern in blessing the merger was whether the deal would result in a safe railroad operation that would serve most of the eastern half of the United States. The Edelman folks knew that reporters, who would talk with FRA officials, would pick up on the government's emphasis on safety.

Consequently the issue of whether the CSX-Conrail merger would result in a safe railroad dominated Edelman's omnibus strategic plan to help CSX through the lengthy merger process. Working with the railroad, the public relations firm staged on-site safety demonstrations for the news media. Edelman was proactive in addressing safety concerns that cities and communities had over the possibility of a greater number of trains that might be running through their towns. Reporters who visited CSX offices were shown how the company planned to merge not only two railroads but also two railroad cultures into a safe new operation.

Interview talking points for CSX spokespersons, backed up by pinpoint data, emphasized how the railroad merger would create the opportunity for American industry to be more cost efficient by shipping large amounts of goods by rail. Savings could even be passed along to consumers. And shipping by rail would reduce the number of trucks on highways. Fewer heavy trucks competing for roadway space with motorists would make it safer for all drivers. Safety was also underscored in briefings for Wall Street analysts in New York and before lawmakers on Capitol Hill in Washington.

In the end, when the FRA approved the merger, the federal agency praised CSX for its emphasis on creating an environment where safety was the No. 1 priority. The government regulators commended CSX for effectively communicating the importance of safety throughout the cultures of both companies and across the entire rail system.

Naturally, because the safety issue was the top priority to the federal watchdog agency and underscored in all their statements to the media, the work done by CSX made positive headlines and dominated the extensive media coverage.

"Successful PR people have a 'service' attitude, as opposed to one based on 'spin control,'" commented longtime Washington, D.C., newspaperman Lyle Denniston. "And successful people understand that 'service' means melding their assistance to the media with loyally serving their client. The two can go together."

> "Successful PR people have a 'service' attitude, as opposed to one based on 'spin control.' And successful people understand that 'service' means melding their assistance to the media with loyally serving their client. The two can go together." — Lyle Denniston, syndicated newspaper reporter

Clearly, in the example of Edelman Public Relations' work with CSX Transportation, service — assistance and a close working relationship with the media — was an essential factor for achieving success.

Overall, when I talked with journalists about the value of media relations to their work in the news business, I found a healthy attitude. Journalists do need people who will give them good stories on a regular basis. They are open to ideas and to covering legitimate and relevant news events. And they believe that public relations people can make a significant contribution to both helping their clients or employers build favorable awareness and provide valuable assistance to the media.

As Scott Simon, the popular host of "Weekend Edition" on National Public Radio, told me, "You are part of an honorable profession. The sanctimony of so many of us journalists aside — I think there is probably about the same proportion of scoundrels to saints in both lines. Cheerfulness counts for a lot."

The first tenet of effective media relations is to passionately embrace the reality that it's a relationship-driven discipline. It really is about who you know in the news media and the level of trust you have developed.

The people assigned to the job of media relations need reporters, and reporters need the stories and resources PR people have to offer. But effective media relations that makes news doesn't begin as a two-way street. It begins with outreach. The challenge in media relations is to find the right journalists and earn their trust — through understanding their needs, providing factual information and adding a healthy measure of good humor.

Only Thing Constant Is Change

There were several sea-change events within a year — starting in late 2004 — that have made a profound impact on journalism and the way news is covered. The events raised important questions, including who is a journalist in today's changing world, and how can we in the business of media relations better communicate with them?

The answers involve learning new techniques. But we need to move quickly, and we have a lot to learn. It begins by letting go of the bygone notion that anyone in the news media is influenced by traditional approaches that have been attempted by media relations people, such as shoveling press materials at the media.

The first event was a tsunami that roared over islands and populated coastal areas in Asia and east Africa, killing tens of thousands of people without warning. The images of the sea devouring whole communities that aired on television news around the world were taken mostly by tourists, not news crews, who were lucky enough to be in higher locations and who had the presence of mind to pick up their digital cameras and shoot.

The second event was the series of terrorist bombings in London, England, on July 7, 2005; and the third was Hurricane Katrina, which devastated New Orleans, Louisiana, and the Gulf Coast.

Each event had the effect of creating a new type of journalist: "citizen journalists," ordinary people like you and me who are witnesses to news in the making. These events shook up the news business and forced the industry to recognize that the forces of news, technology and reality have altered the face of journalism forever.

For public relations people, the events presented new opportunities and new methods of communicating more influentially than ever through the media. Media relations methods are evolving seemingly at light speed. The message is clear: Stop mailing out all those news releases and watch the trends.

When the July 7 bombs detonated in the London tube, eyewitness video — the only video available of the explosions — was taken by passengers who switched their cell or mobile phones to video mode and took dramatic pictures. When editors at BBC Television news became aware of the grainy yet spellbinding video, the decision was immediately made to put those images on the air as quickly as possible. The riveting video was broadcast around the world, driving home the horror of terrorism for many of us.

"The London bombs of 7/7 changed the business of broadcast news forever," Jon Williams, a senior editor at BBC Television News, wrote me in an e-mail. "For the first time, the audience became 'citizen journalists' en-masse by sending their mobile phone pictures — stills and video — by SMS [cell phone text messaging] and e-mail.

"Potentially everyone is a journalist. If something goes wrong — if something happens — someone, somewhere will capture it on a mobile phone. Whether it's the queues outside Heathrow airport because of the British Airways strike, or a bus driver caught abusing a passenger, there's no hiding place for organizations any more."

Within hours of the July 7 bombings, the BBC was alerting viewers and listeners about special Internet links where witnesses could upload any pictures or video they had captured. Response was overwhelming, and the venerable British news institution quickly found their coverage ahead of competitors, all because their viewers had become their reporters.

It is my personal observation that this almost instant partnership between an audience and the BBC speaks volumes about citizens' devotion to and respect for the news operations of the British Broadcasting Corporation. It is a loyalty that today eludes television news organizations in the United States, partly because there are far more choices for getting news in America.

There's a larger reason for the audience disenfranchisement in the United States. So many broadcast news outfits in America — focused on delivering news that is consultant- and formula-driven — have isolated themselves from what is relevant and meaningful in their respective communities and from their audiences.

As many media relations specialists know all too well, it's often a challenge to reach the right person at a TV or radio newsroom. For the average citizen, who may have a legitimate news story but lacks the unlisted telephone numbers, it's nearly impossible. So while the local "Eyewitness News" may promote themselves as "on your side" and "working harder for you," they have not, in all honesty, worked to reach out and earn the loyalty of their audiences. That isolationist behavior by broadcast newsrooms is beginning to turn around out of necessity for survival.

A couple of months after the terrorist bombings in London, an enormous hurricane named Katrina struck the Gulf Coast and the city of New Orleans. The devastation was beyond comprehension. As fierce winds blew and the storm surge leveled towns along the coast, amateur photographers, armed with their MiniDV video cameras and digital still cameras normally intended for home movies and pictures of the kids, captured effects of the historic storm.

A few television news organizations appealed to these citizen journalists to share their pictures, and even though the response was not as overwhelming when compared to the London bombings, what the U.S. television news organizations received was some of the most graphic and dramatic video and digital still photos of the storm and its aftermath.

Jerry Kay, general manager of Environmental News Network, points to the fact that a news assignment that once required a $20,000 video camera can now be reported using a cell phone.

"Amazingly, some of the first and most striking images of Hurricane Katrina were actually captured by cell phones," he said. "Anyone can be a producer and use video as a way of communicating a mission, conveying a message or sharing a passion with the world."

What caught my attention during the Katrina disaster was a fresh openness of the news media to accepting visual coverage from ordinary folks, like you and me. Even if you were a public relations person who had outstanding and relevant video of a news event, the media would likely be open to airing your pictures with full knowledge that you might be working to promote a client.

This was the same television news media that was up in arms a few months earlier after it was revealed that Ketchum Public Relations had produced video news releases or VNRs that were distributed to television newsrooms across the country to promote the No Child Left Behind or NCLB law on behalf of the Department of Education. The whole scheme to sell NCLB, which included journalist payola, was subsequently labeled "covert propaganda" by the Government Accountability Office. Just a year earlier, Ketchum had a government contract to produce video news releases to hype the Bush administration's new approach to Medicare, and that too blew up in a controversy over whether to use taxpayer money to create fake news reports in support of a government agenda.

Video news releases have been sent out by organizations for decades as a way to get specific messages and images on television newscasts, and if the story was good, it had a chance of getting on the air. But the No Child Left Behind and Medicare stunts had the effect of poisoning the well for the whole concept of legitimate video news releases. Overnight television news operations got skittish and stopped airing them for a while, until the flap cooled off. Television news has a short memory and will air worthwhile and appealing video, regardless of the source.

Incidentally the No Child Left Behind scandal was not limited to bogus VNRs. The Education Department paid nationally syndicated television show commentator Armstrong Williams $241,000 to help promote the Bush administration's education reform law on the air.

USA Today reported that the campaign required Williams "to regularly comment on NCLB during the course of his broadcasts." Once again, the money was funneled through Ketchum Public Relations.

Such stories of payola, domestic propaganda and bad judgment aside, newer opportunities to get your messages on television newscasts are opening, especially if you invest the time to develop a genuine, timely news story — the sort of story the media will want.

The openness of the media to reconsider and accept images from outside sources during the London bombings and Katrina signaled a change that merits notice by the public relations industry. While the days of a traditional video news release may well be nearly over, television news will air video from outside sources that is — and this is very important — timely, relevant and, most of all, compelling. The more exciting the video, the better.

A "seismic change," as journalists are calling it, in the news business is on a roll and gaining momentum, driven mostly by technology that has made every instant a news cycle, younger audiences who are bombarded by more sources of information and by leaders in the mass media who are concerned about economic storm clouds for the industry. In an industry where money often dictates the quality of news reporting we see, executives are worried. Faced with competition for advertising dollars and competition from cable and the Internet, the traditional media is scrambling to assure a viable future.

"Hold on," you may say. "This sounds familiar ... countless other industries faced similar challenges and shakeouts around 2000." You would be correct, and those warning signs were out there then for the news business. It just took news executives a little longer to figure out that the earth was shifting out from underneath their feet. Some are still working on it.

CBS News is a prime example of a traditional mainstream news organization slow to change and searching for its audience.

Joe Gandelman of *The Moderate Voice* blog has written, "The biggest issue facing CBS is whether — and how — it can adjust a venerable news institution to the reality that we're living in the 21st century, and it may be time to explore changes in form as well as personnel. The same style, format and pacing that worked for the World War II and baby boomer generations may not be best for the MTV and iPod generations."

Ever-changing audience expectations, the merging of technologies and the instantaneous 24-hour news cycle have only increased the amount of news and information available to consumers and has decreased the importance of traditional media.

For the news business, the jury is out — primarily because you and I are the jury — and we are faced with many new sources these days to get all the news and information we desire. To make matters worse, surveys show that we are also losing trust in the traditional news media.

Dan Gillmor, a former reporter for the *The Mercury News* in San Jose and pioneer Web journalist, or blogger, said, "It's painful to watch a business I care so much about commit slow suicide this way. But the financial writing is increasingly on the wall for the industry that simply can't figure out how to handle its challenges." Yet Gillmor and other journalists see this change bringing tremendous new opportunities for more effective communications between public relations people and the news media.

Gillmor, who regularly offers sage advice to PR people, writes in his blog, *Bayosphere*, that for media relations and PR people, "traditional methods must give way to different kinds of conversations."

"But the key word here is 'conversation' — and the first rule is that you have to listen. That's why companies should encourage comments from those various constituencies, publicly and privately. A conversation doesn't mean total transparency, but it does mean a willingness to listen. We all have plenty to learn."

A study by the Annenberg Public Policy Center has shown that the American public is split about evenly on whether news organizations usually get their facts straight. The center quotes Geneva Overholser, a journalism professor and former *Washington Post* ombudsman, as saying, "This study reveals a worrisome divide between the public's view of journalism and journalists' own views of their work." In other words, reporters may think their work is sound and important, but we may not agree.

The media center at the American Press Institute started watching these trends long before the July 7 bombings and Katrina. They have pulled together a group of visionary journalists to watch the evolution of the news business, and the goal is to try to make sense of the trends. The media center's project is called We Media. The "we" is all of us: you, me and everyone else.

Their research is fascinating and begins at a very high perspective. They have found that only three communications exist. The first two of the three communication media predate technology and have mutually exclusive characteristics.

"*Interpersonal* communications," according to the media center, "is the first communication medium. We commonly know it as one person talking to one other person." That manner of communicating has been around for a long time. Its hallmark is that what's shared reflects a unique mix of interests, and "each partisan equally shares control of the content."

"The second communication medium is what the mass of people colloquially refer to as 'media.' It is the *mass medium.*" Newspapers and broadcasters fall into this category, because one person has sole control of the content. Other vehicles of the mass medium are theater, books, royal decrees and speeches.

Here's the exciting part, especially when learning how to be more effective at media relations: There is a new communication medium that doesn't have the mutually exclusive advantages and disadvantages of the two previous forms.

The *new medium* of communication, according to the media center, "can simultaneously send an individually tailored message, edition or program to everyone on a mass scale. And, it lets every participant equally share control," leveling the playing field between publisher and consumer. Either can be both. That's where journalism is headed.

Web sites are not vehicles of this new medium because, for the most part, they merely push mostly passive information at an audience. In the case of Web sites of newspapers, magazines and broadcasters, their sites are nothing more than "shovelware" from the mass medium. That means stories are shoveled or pushed in one direction — our direction — hoping we'll be interested. In fact most Web sites are either passive, archival, or shovelware, or a combination of all three. It's not a particularly appealing brew for today's more discriminating online public.

Blogs — online journals — are something else entirely. Blogs have grown from an outlet for tech-savvy geeks to an increasingly influential level of communications. Blogs are interactive. You can give feedback, and you can comment. In fact we are seeing that the more popular blogs are the more interactive ones that give readers a voice. That's participatory journalism, and the concept has caught the news media's attention, big-time.

We are seeing news-oriented bloggers keeping mainstream journalists on their toes by carefully digging into the background of controversial stories and providing another level of fact-checking. Bloggers have done the job the more traditional reporters failed to tackle on stories, such as the use of white phosphorus as a chemical weapon by U.S. troops in Iraq or the provenance of the letters claiming to be from George W. Bush's commander in the National Guard — the flawed story that brought down the credibility of CBS News anchorman Dan Rather.

Blogs are new media and have become a popular, powerful way of influencing reporters, columnists and editors. Each day respected journalists, from Frank Rich at *The New York Times* to Brit Hume at Fox News, quote something they've read in a blog.

So here's the difference between the mass medium and the new medium: An editor today can eyeball all 100 stories that he packages into his "one-to-many" mass medium newspaper edition. But tomorrow, when his newspaper might be packaging a different 90 stories for each reader, he's no longer a chef making a meal, but rather providing a menu of information. It is up to us to decide what's relevant and what isn't. That's new media.

There's the big opportunity for people in media relations: This seismic change in the news business opens the door for delivering our stories to the media and making news, so long as our stories are more legitimate, more timely, more relevant and more compelling. Public relations people have the chance to join in as citizen journalists and provide the media with material, provided it's a real news story that we pitch to a specific reporter or news organization. No one is paying attention to self-serving, boring and fluffy news announcements. The competition for audiences is too fierce. These are exciting new ways of making news.

While we hear journalists say they are open to these stories from outside sources, their message is also that we need to embrace new styles and technology for communicating with the media.

- Get away from traditional news releases if for no other reason than because reporters are buried in too many of them.

- Only hold news conferences when we really, really have something important to say, and even then, find credible ways of covering our own news conferences for reporters who can't make it because of increased work demands.

- Watch the signs and remain open to emerging new trends in technology, like blogs, as a delivery method of updating the media with razor-edge timeliness.

The invitation from the media has been extended to those of us who make our living placing stories about our clients and employers in the news media. The media is perhaps more open than ever to partnering with us so long as we play by their rules and understand what they require. They make their livings reporting timely, legitimate news stories. Give them what they need to make news.

It's the "News Media"

At first blush you may think this is not a big deal or just nitpicking terminology. You may be right. Then again, perhaps not.

The difference between *press* and *media* is subtle but important. Understanding the difference is important if you are to be effective in media relations. At the very least it shows you are savvy about the news media.

The term *press* originated from the printing press and has been associated with the newspaper business for decades. A caricature of the press evolved in black and white motion pictures years ago of reporters with large "press" cards stuck in the brims of their hats, sometimes lugging big cameras that fired off golf ball-sized flash bulbs. Those days are over and gone.

Nonetheless hundreds of Web sites for organizations large and small still refer visitors to their "press room." Such use of the word screams at site visitors that this is an organization that is … well, not keeping up with the times. Incidentally, a press room is where the printing presses are located to physically print a paper.

To many journalists your knowledge of the difference between press and media quietly says something about you and your level of knowledge and awareness in media relations. I've known some broadcast reporters who were offended when someone called them the press. They are not, so why call them that? It may not be a deal breaker as to whether they do a story, but it's the sort of thing that can get you off on the wrong foot with a reporter. You may never know what a broadcast newsperson or any journalist thinks about being called the press. Play it safe and professional.

Now you may be thinking, "Hey, wait a minute, Henderson. I hear reporters using the word *press* and *press release* all the time. What gives?!"

Well, it's their industry, and they can call it and themselves whatever they wish. My point is that in this era of 24-hour cable news programs, up-to-the-minute Internet news services, split-second news cycles, emerging technology and rapidly changing methods of instantly reporting the news from virtually anywhere on earth, the term *press* is passé and about as old-fashioned as an old typewriter. Heck, even the definition of *reporter* is up for grabs these days now that video taken on your cell phone might air on a television newscast. You might be a tax attorney one minute, take history-making video on your phone the next and end up being called a citizen journalist by the end of the day. So let's try to be as clear as possible.

If we are going to do an effective job at media relations in this fast-changing environment, let's work to set the pace. Using old terminology is neither hip nor cool and just might be a turnoff to a 20-something out there who is creating tomorrow's world of journalism.

News media, or simply the *media*, refers to the organizations and the people who cover, report, edit, direct and produce the news, from that found in television and radio to that in newspapers, magazines and the Internet.

> *News media*, or simply the *media*, refers to the organizations and the people who cover, report, edit, direct and produce the news, from that found in television and radio to that in newspapers, magazines and the Internet.

Today's journalists are members of the news media, not necessarily the press.

Ratings, Ratings, Ratings

Effective media relations in today's world mandates that communicators — including public relations people who deal with the media — work harder than ever to understand how stories occur and how news happens. Communications people also need to try, whenever possible, to stay ahead of trends in news coverage.

Public relations people need "a reality check," said Linda Ellerbee, a television reporter, anchor and producer with over three decades of distinguished work. "We are in the middle of a seismic shift in how we, and the rest of the world, receive our news," she said.

Today's news in general, and television news in particular, is more focused on immediacy than accuracy, Ellerbee said.

Neal Shapiro, executive producer of "Dateline NBC" for many years, agrees. He told during a dinner in New York that television news is solely about "ratings, ratings, ratings." That's how his program decides what stories to air. Whatever story will attract the biggest audience is the story that television news will report.

Of course what he's saying is that "ratings, ratings, ratings" translates into "money, money, money" for NBC.

Gone are the days when the purpose was purely to inform. Instead the quest for ratings and the resulting money directly drives editorial content.

Consider stories coming out of small communities that have taken on worldwide importance, such as the Laci Peterson case — a tragic local story in Modesto, California, that included murder, adultery, betrayal and pregnancy. The pregnant 27-year-old woman's husband, Scott Peterson, was found guilty of killing his wife and unborn child.

Among other facts, it was disclosed that he was having an affair with another woman and played golf the day after the murders.

The case spawned at least a dozen books and scores of Web sites, many devoted to the memory of Laci Peterson.

Although it lacked any real international relevance, the case became international news for months, at times capturing headlines ahead of terrorism, wars and other major world events. The story's elevated status is not surprising, because the often-scurrilous details of the Peterson case captured bigger audiences for the news media.

The same principle applied in the case of Alabama teenager Natalee Holloway, who went missing while vacationing in Aruba. Coverage of her disappearance pushed aside headlines out of the Iraq war, the economy and world events for weeks. Even two months after the girl vanished, MSNBC's news personality Rita Cosby still persisted in covering the story of the missing teenager even though there were no new leads and even as Hurricane Katrina slammed into New Orleans.

After media interest in Hurricane Katrina waned, Cosby continued her stories about the missing teen for months, even when Cosby had nothing new to report. If her reports hadn't gotten ratings for her bosses at MSNBC, she wouldn't have spent so much airtime on the story. Besides, who could blame a reporter for wanting to camp out on Aruba, hoping for a break in the case? Not me.

You can see that today's media environment is curious and at times difficult. In capturing attention for what we have to say, telling our story and making news, we face stiff competition. There are new challenges at every turn. Someone or some event of the day is always out there with a sexier angle or more timely approach.

To stay ahead of this game, you need to know the players. "My one piece of advice for people in the PR industry," said Lisa Guernsey of *The New York Times*, "would be to get to know the reporters to whom you are pitching. Know their beats. Know their most recent stories. Know the personalities of the sections that they write for."

Linda Ellerbee offered eight tips for public relations people looking to get savvier when working with the media:

1. Remember that a public relations professional's job is to change things. A reporter's job is not.

2. If you are simply trying to raise publicity, buy an ad. Remember that reporters need to see the context of your message.

3. Just because you are worthy, it doesn't mean you are newsworthy. Find the story within the theme.

4. Know what reporters are looking for before you pitch them a story.

5. Make a friend in the news business. They know what a good story looks like, and their input can be valuable.

6. Never lie to a reporter. It will ruin your reputation.

7. Don't contact a reporter with a full story unless they invite you to do so. Give them a simple, to-the-point summary on initial contact.

8. Remember that good reporters love good PR people. A healthy, professional relationship makes everyone's job easier.

At my strategic communications agency, I coached our younger team members about media relations by saying the team members either needed to make friends and contacts in the news media or learn to accept rejection gracefully.

People in media relations must stay open to new approaches and ideas. They need to be aware of the media's never-ending appetite for some new and different twist on a story, the current flavor of the day. And they should never take it personally when they get turned down.

Getting your story before the news media can be done, but a level of smart planning and hard work are required to really understand how the news media operates and what its needs are. Effective media relations begins with understanding what reporters need for a story and then finding imaginative and timely news angles to get their attention.

Media relations today is a whole new ball game. At times it's fiercely competitive, and you've got to keep up with the game in order to score points.

One Size Does Not Fit All

It wasn't that long ago that newspaper editors and broadcast news producers sat in ivory towers and ran stories that they believed their broad audiences would need to know about. Those were the days — before government deregulation and all of today's choices for news — when we dutifully sat down each evening, usually in our living rooms, to watch the 30-minute newscasts of ABC, NBC and CBS.

In many communities across the country, this was how Americans learned what happened in the world that day — or at least what the news decision makers in New York thought we should know.

There's the legendary story that on the day that the Three Mile Island nuclear reactor nearly melted down in March 1979 in Pennsylvania, CBS Evening News chose to lead with a story about Britain's Queen Elizabeth because the producers in New York thought that, in the realm of world events, the queen was a more important story. They were wrong.

Today nobody remembers the story about the queen, but a lot of people still remember Three Mile Island.

It was a pivotal moment — a wake-up call — for CBS News. Viewers and affiliate stations alike responded that the news division was out of touch with its audience, and it was.

Most media decision makers today are keenly aware of who their primary audiences are and what kind of news is most likely to appeal to them. The news business today is formula-driven to satisfy the perceived news and interest appetites of specific groups and demographics.

It's not only "All The News That's Fit To Print," as *The New York Times* says. It's also the news that you are likely to be interested in and talk about with your friends and colleagues. That's how popular newspapers and broadcast news programs become even more successful: by focusing on stories that appeal to audiences. The purpose of journalism now is to sell newspapers and magazines and build audiences for broadcast stations, networks and cable channels.

The kind of story, for example, that runs on the front page of one daily newspaper might not appeal to editors at another newspaper in the same city. For all kinds of reasons — political, cultural, economic, demographic and/or social — each media outlet has its own primary target audiences.

USA Today, for example, has a style geared to business people on the run, with incisively written and very timely stories encapsulated in as few words as possible. *USA Today* wants to make sure you learned about it first from them.

Its detractors have called *USA Today* "the McPaper" because, like fast food, you can consume it quickly and there is little nourishment or depth. Some of the paper's features amount to little more than nuggets of information that editors believe their readers want. But *USA Today* has been highly successful for over two decades, because it knows and focuses on specific audiences.

USA Today has essentially reinvented the way news is presented today, using crisp color and concise editorial content, graphics and visuals. The paper has forced other media decision makers to rethink their broad marketing appeal and re-evaluate how they fit on the competitive landscape in order to stay in business.

It's not surprising that the type of in-depth and sometimes lengthy news analysis you find in *The New York Times* won't appear in *USA Today*. Both newspapers are popular, well-written, and respected, yet each has an entirely different approach to covering news. Each has its own primary audience. So while any news organization — whether newspaper or broadcast or magazine or online — wants to capture the largest audience possible, they have carefully defined primary audiences, and they work hard to feel the pulse of those audiences.

Today's effective media relations professional must also have his or her finger on that pulse, evaluating the journalistic trends and even the politics of several different news organizations in order to find the right home for a favorable story. A story that would be perfect for National Public Radio might be dismissed by the more conservative Fox News.

Beyond the more traditional news media is today's 24-hour news cycle and the instant reach of Internet news sites and news-oriented blogs. We live in the age of instant news coverage, when a story carried on the Associated Press wire in America can appear on the Web site of a newspaper in Melbourne, Australia, in the blink of an eye.

So, in media relations, how do you find the best place for your story?

- *Target.* Make a list of communities or cities or places where you want news of your organization to appear. Include trade magazines, and think about whether your story might cross over and appeal to trades in more than one industry sector. Call it your "shopping list" because, as when we go to the mall, sometimes our shopping list is a little grander than our budget.

- *Get smart.* Read up on specific publications and news outlets on your shopping list. Have they covered your type of story before? What are their political influences or overtones? What are the general demographics of their audience? What sort of depth might they devote to a story about your organization? Believe it or not, the *The National Inquirer* may be a terrific way to reach an enormous audience segment with a consumer-oriented story that might not appeal to editors at the *Los Angeles Times*.

- *Shoot high.* Just because *The Wall Street Journal* has never before reported on your industry sector doesn't mean they are not interested in your company. As head of corporate communications at Gulfstream Aerospace, I found that while most business reporters hadn't been interested for years in a stereotypical story pitch about the merits of business aircraft, they were attracted to a skillfully crafted story pitch about the hot trend among corporations of buying ultra-expensive, ultra-long-range business jets.

When I invited select groups of top-level mainstream journalists from around the world to experience a flight aboard the $40 million Gulfstream V at 50,000 feet, far above all other aircraft traffic, and at a speed faster than most commercial airliners, it always guaranteed a great story, sometimes on the front page. They always mentioned one of our key selling points: The Gulfstream V is the world's longest range, high-performance business jet. The same story angle about the Gulfstream V appeared in every major publication and television news outlet around the world, and during that time, orders for the new aircraft increased 443 percent.

In today's style of media relations, part of the trick to capturing a reporter's attention is to begin by identifying the right media outlet for your story, with keen attention paid to placement opportunities at online news sites and news-oriented blogs.

Be Friendly, Be Funny
and Be Honest

We are in a new era for both the news media and media relations people ... and there are high hopes on both sides.

The news media has in recent years been faced with its own concerns over credibility. The industry has suffered more than its share of figurative black eyes. There have been revelations of reporters making up stories, fabricating details and reporting interviews that never took place, sometimes with imaginary people.

There are many examples.

A reporter named Janet Cooke at *The Washington Post* won a Pulitzer Prize for a story about an 8-year-old heroin addict. It was subsequently revealed that there was no such person, and Cooke resigned from the paper and was stripped of the Pulitzer.

At the venerable *New York Times*, it was discovered that Jayson Blair, a rising star in the newsroom, had made up dozens of stories, sometimes plagiarizing the work of other reporters or just downright lying in his writing.

The reputation of CBS News was shaken to the core when anchorman Dan Rather broadcast allegations on the program "60 Minutes II" about George Bush's National Guard service 30 years earlier. It turned out that Rather's report, which aired during the 2004 presidential campaign, was based on documents of unsubstantiated and questionable origin. Faced with intense criticism from the White House and conservative bloggers as well as several investigations, Rather announced within a month that he would step down as anchorman of the CBS Evening News. CBS's "60 Minutes II" was canceled soon after.

Fallout from the intense and loud criticism from a small but well-orchestrated ultra-conservative group that supported President George W. Bush's re-election efforts sent ripples of fear through the news media at a time during the hot presidential race when some news organizations were looking into reports of ballot-box tampering and other irregularities. The media became "gun shy," as one journalist told me, of further investigative reporting.

It may well have been that by going after Dan Rather over a story that was fundamentally true but based on unverified documents, conservative groups managed to not only control but also manipulate the news media from covering an even larger story.

Then there was Stephen Glass, who admitted making up sources and whole news stories while a staff reporter for *The New Republic* magazine.

The technology bubble of the late 1990s was also a sobering experience for the media. Many reporters were sucked into the hype and convinced by the overblown claims of tech's high flyers. There was fierce competition between news organizations to report the latest tech industry developments, even when they lacked substance and validation. In the end, most if not all of the claims turned out to be nothing more than hot air.

The irresponsible or unwise actions of a few people in the media have at times injured the reputations of otherwise outstanding and conscientious news organizations.

In most cases respected news organizations acted quickly to understand what went wrong with their internal standards of checks and balances and took corrective action. So what we have today is a news media that has expeditiously conducted a responsible job of re-examination and is keenly aware of its responsibility as the guardians of fair, accurate, responsible and balanced reporting. Traditional news organizations must regain audience trust. Consequently the transparency of news organizations as they go about their trade of journalism is a growing trend.

The New York Times, for instance, hired Byron Calame, a journalist from the more conservative *Wall Street Journal*, as its people editor. His role is advocate for the paper's readers — the crucial audience often ignored in newsgathering.

Calame regularly takes an unbiased look at questions of fairness and accuracy in the *Times* and freely reports his conclusions on the paper's Sunday op-ed page. His reports are unvarnished. It is not uncommon for him to write that the paper made a mistake on a story. He has even taken reporters and editors to task over their handling of a story.

In one case, Calame wrote, "One of the real tests of journalistic integrity is being fair to someone who might be best described by a four-letter word. *The New York Times* flunked such a test in rejecting a demand by Geraldo Rivera of Fox News for a correction of a sentence about him in a column by the paper's chief television critic."

Calame also has a blog to focus on matters that aren't appropriate for his column in the Sunday op-ed pages, or won't fit into them. His direct telephone number, e-mail and mailing addresses are all included for easy access by readers.

He and the *Times* have recognized that the future of the news industry is participatory journalism, defined by the Media Center at the American Press Institute as "the act of a citizen, or group of citizens, playing an active role in the process of collecting, reporting, analyzing and disseminating news and information."

Many other news organizations have beefed up editorial scrutiny of stories and fact-checking as best they can within budget constraints and staffing cutbacks. Internally questions are asked if a story seems too dramatic, too bold, too cutting-edge. Outwardly the media has learned to smell hype coming their way from several miles away and avoid it like the plague.

Therein lies a basic challenge of media relations today: how to credibly communicate what your organization wants to say to its public audiences or stakeholders via the media while, at the same time, understanding the ever-changing and often trendy needs and methods of the news business. Media relations methods that seemed to work last month may not achieve any results today.

Media relations requires persistence and fresh approaches. It certainly is not in any organization's best interest to adopt an attitude toward the media that might be perceived as arrogant or pushy.

Veteran Washington, D.C., reporter Lyle Denniston said, "A 'savior of the world' or 'working for the good of all of us' complex is always unconvincing. I am never persuaded that, as General Motors goes, so goes the nation.

"The competition of conflicting private interests reflects the openness of American society. As a journalist, however, I say just tell me what you're up to; you do not need to assume that I agree with your agenda in order to expect me to treat it with professional respect."

Many journalists simply are skeptical of public relations people, perhaps fearing hidden agendas. "PR people need to be less controlling and manipulative," said veteran ABC and CBS network television correspondent John Laurence.

In many ways, communications with the news media mirrors behavior. An organization that dodges facts and manipulates issues will ultimately erode whatever credibility it may have. On the other hand a leading organization in any given industry will be identified by how well it communicates with the media in an open, candid and professional manner.

Arthur Page, vice president of public relations at AT&T for two decades and the public relations professional after whom the Arthur W. Page Society was named, wrote, "All business in a democratic country begins with public permission and exists by public approval."

Page viewed public relations as the art of developing understanding and communicating character — both corporate and individual.

This vision, albeit somewhat halcyon by nature in today's world, was an outgrowth of Page's belief in humanism and freedom as America's guiding characteristics and as preconditions for capitalism.

Whenever I hear an organization talk about best practices, I am reminded of Page's statements on corporate behavior and the role of public relations. Best practices for many corporations and not-for-profit groups has too often become an elaborate exercise in developing flowery rhetoric and, in the end, fairly unimaginative and empty proclamations that some executives recite with what can only be described as a divine glow, as if the tone of their voice will make the declarations sound deeper than they are. What Page said, by sharp contrast, is clear and pragmatic and remains rock solid to this day.

Page believed idealistically that the successful organization must shape its character in concert with that of the nation. It must operate in the public interest, manage for the long term and make customer satisfaction its primary goal.

"Real success, both for big business and the public," Page said, "lies in large enterprise conducting itself in the public interest and in such a way that the public will give it succinct freedom to serve effectively."

Page viewed media relations as the art of developing, understanding and communicating corporate and individual character, and he practiced seven principles of public relations management as a means of implementing his philosophy.

Today the seven Page Principles that help to define integrity in media relations are deceptively simple:

1. *Tell the truth.* Let the public know what's happening, and provide an accurate picture of the company's character, ideals and practices.

2. *Prove it with action.* Public perception of an organization is determined 90 percent by what it does and 10 percent by talking.

3. *Listen to the customer.* To serve the company well, understand what the public wants and needs. Keep top decision makers and other employees informed about public reaction to company products, policies and practices.

4. *Manage for tomorrow.* Anticipate public reaction and eliminate practices that create difficulties. Generate goodwill.

5. *Realize a company's true character is expressed by its people.* The strongest opinions — good or bad — about a company are shaped by the words and deeds of its employees. As a result, every employee — active or retired — is involved with public relations. It is the responsibility of corporate communications to support each employee's capability and desire to be an honest, knowledgeable ambassador to customers, friends, shareholders and public officials.

6. *Conduct public relations as if the whole company depends on it.* Corporate relations is a management function. No corporate strategy should be implemented without considering its impact on the public. The public relations professional is a policymaker capable of handling a wide range of corporate communications activities.

7. *Remain calm, patient and good-humored.* Lay the groundwork for public relations miracles with consistent, calm and reasoned attention to information and contacts. When a crisis arises, remember that cool heads communicate best.

Linda Stasi, longtime columnist for the *New York Post*, candidly sums it up this way: "Be honest, be friendly and be funny. The best PR people are people who are honest, and in many, many cases are people who have become my friends."

> "Be honest, be friendly and be funny. The best PR people are people who are honest, and in many, many cases are people who have become my friends." — Linda Stasi, columnist, *New York Post*

Honesty and integrity are qualities that leaders and those responsible for media relations need to own and communicate tirelessly throughout their organizations, through words and deeds. Effective media relations begins with words as well as actions that are accurate, comprehensive and formed by integrity.

Here Come the Lemmings

Ever wonder why so many stories you first read in this morning's paper show up later on the evening television newscast with little or no update? And have you ever wondered why that interesting story you heard on National Public Radio a couple of weeks ago is just now making it into the newspaper?

There exists a pecking order in America's news media. Let's draw an analogy to the much-maligned Alaskan lemming, the rodent creature that, according to popular myth, runs in packs, first in one direction and then the other, seemingly without rhyme or reason — even if headed over a cliff. Ah, but there is rhyme and reason in the news media. There are some in the pack more trusted than others.

Despite all the appearances of competition between America's print and broadcast news media, what is covered by the news media and the style in which it is covered is largely influenced by how someone else in the news media has previously reported the story. For lack of a better description, let's call this the *lemming effect*. It's all about leadership — and, perhaps, lack of it — and a hierarchy of influence within the news media.

This effect shows up most often in the area of enterprise news reporting — the side of journalism that requires digging for unusual angles, finding outstanding sources and unearthing award-winning stories. Enterprise stories are generally found first on National Public Radio news programs or on the pages of major daily newspapers. Television news, in most cases, has accepted the default job of reporting the follow-up on the original story — and making it as sensational as possible, often to give the impression that they came up with the story even though they did not.

Here's how it works: Even though television news has been around a half a century and is perhaps the most powerful of the news media, the decision makers of TV news are an insecure group. With few exceptions, they will not consider running any story that smacks of controversy until it has appeared first in print, either in a newspaper or on a wire service.

One motivator for this approach is an unspoken fear that a story might upset an advertiser. Advertisers rule. News coverage rolls over.

At the morning story planning sessions at each of the television networks in New York, producers sit around the room with copies of that day's *New York Times* in their laps. What appears in the morning *Times* often influences what America will see nine hours later on the evening television news.

It is no different in local television newsrooms in communities around the country. What will appear on the evening news is influenced by that morning's local newspaper. And stories that appeared overnight on the Associated Press broadcast wire service often provide ideas for local coverage later that day. Consequently much of what viewers see at the end of the day is recycled old news, often from the day before.

Sure, there are exceptions, such as breaking news. The network news operations have wars, natural disasters and news conferences to cover during the day. Local news covers fires, car wrecks and local news conferences. But even then television news is astonishingly slow to update a breaking story.

Remember when parts of the northeast, including New York City, were hit by a massive electrical power failure one hot August afternoon in 2003? Television news was all over the story. But the next afternoon, CNN was still recycling video about the hardships people had faced 24 hours earlier.

On the second day of such a widespread power outage, a viewer might expect CNN and the others to tell us the latest news. Not so. They were still rehashing what happened the day before, showing and re-showing video of people walking home in a darkened city even though it was a day later, and the story offered completely new and different news angles.

And it has always been thus. As a young network news correspondent starting out at CBS News, I was counseled by Zeke Segal, a highly respected veteran assignment editor, to never get ahead of the story. He advised to always validate any major story by how it was approached or covered by the print news media. "We are and will always be the reaction side of journalism," he said referring to broadcast news.

Sadly that's still true today, despite amazing technological advances in newsgathering. The effect is compounded by the fact that contemporary television news is entertainment-driven. In many cities, "entertainment news" has the distinct flavor of Amateur Hour. Far too many of today's television anchors are nothing more than actors or readers with no journalistic training or credentials. Behind the scenes are news producers and interns with varying degrees of experience who are learning on the job. It is not surprising that the accuracy of reporting and the quality of writing on local television news are mediocre.

It is also not surprising then that TV newspeople feel safer about airing a story once they've seen it in print somewhere.

Even though impressive technological resources enable them to cover the news virtually anywhere on the planet, television newspeople do little original or enterprising reporting, focusing instead on recycling whatever appeared in the newspapers or wire services. Even breaking news, with its often-dramatic visuals, is generally covered in more depth by the print media and radio.

Now what about National Public Radio and newspapers? Whether at NPR headquarters in Washington or at their local stations around the country, a hallmark of National Public Radio is responsible, comprehensive and compelling original journalistic reporting. Many die-hard NPR listeners have forgotten the number of times they have been late to morning meetings at work because of sitting in their cars to hear the end of some story on the radio. They're called *parking-lot moments,* when you're arrived at your destination and remain glued to the car radio to hear the last of a riveting story.

National Public Radio is one of America's most influential news sources, and they have the audience numbers to prove it. NPR audience statistics will often eclipse those of major network television news programs.

Among those often spellbound by some story we hear on NPR are newspaper reporters, who are looking for good story ideas. If an NPR story catches their interest, there's a good chance they will write about it. And then, of course, the TV newspeople will read about it in the paper, and the lemming effect by the news media will continue.

In media relations, a basic objective is to get your story before target audiences as responsibly and accurately as possible through the credible and influential conduit of the news media. You also want a reasonable degree of control over the story. And of course, you hope for good coverage. Consequently television news is not the first place to take your story if you hope to have it air in an accurate manner.

You want to capitalize on the perception that when the media reports about you, you are seen as a leader. Consequently, when possible and appropriate in practicing media relations, work first with public radio stations, commercial news/talk radio stations, newspapers and wire services. There you generally will find today's best level of journalism, which will lead to more credibility and influence on important audiences.

Rules of Engagement

Earned Versus Paid Media

Buy an ad, and that's *paid media* — just another word for advertising.

Talk a reporter into doing a story, and that's *earned media*. You went out, pitched a story and earned the coverage. Good for you!

Here's a little exercise: Carefully read the front page of a daily newspaper or a magazine. As you do, consider that at least half of the news content was influenced by a professional public relations person who worked with a journalist to get a client involved in a story, either by providing expert perspective and being quoted or by providing background and information that brought credibility to the story.

Kiehl's Since 1851 — maker of hair and skin-care products — is an example of a successful company that doesn't advertise. In fact, in an industry where competitors spend millions on paid advertisements, Kiehl's business model is driven by legitimate coverage in the news media. What they have is a team of smart media relations professionals.

Kiehl's has learned to use media relations so effectively to enhance its trendy image and to sell products that its distinctive methods have taken on what might best be described as a form of art. Many of today's hottest personalities, from actors to athletes, swear by the products. When competitors place an expensive display ad in a magazine, Kiehl's may have a story and photos of celebrities who use their products in the same magazine. Which approach do you think will generate more consumer interest?

When I spoke with Susan Towers, Kiehl's vice president of global communications, she said their customers have expressed how much they value media stories about the company's products. Consequently news coverage and third-party endorsements of Kiehl's products have become an integral part of the company's success.

Another company to find big results in media coverage has been Starz Entertainment Group. Starz engaged Brodeur Public Relations to help prepare for the launch of VONGO, a new subscription-based video download service, at the 2006 Consumer Electronics Show — the largest electronics show in the United States. With VONGO, consumers use their broadband Internet connections to download from a large library of motion pictures and other video content — including first-run feature films — for playback on Windows-based PCs, laptops and select portable media devices as well as on televisions. The movies and videos can be watched wherever and whenever a VONGO subscriber desires.

Starz was the first among its competitors to provide such a service, and naturally a company goal was to become one of the top stories at the Consumer Electronics Show, an event where the national news media reports on the latest developments.

The team at Brodeur, an agency that specializes in high technology, knew that in the trendy world of high tech, a story about valuable digital content for consumers would be a popular news angle for reporters, certainly as much so as the newest electronic gizmos. The story was also appealing because Starz had partnered with Microsoft and because VONGO had received third-party endorsement from key industry analysts.

For Brodeur, however, time was limited. They had 10 weeks to develop a media relations approach that was right on target. The Brodeur people focused on their media contacts and conducted briefings with a handful of specific national journalists who might be interested, including The Associated Press. AP newswire coverage can be the catalyst for dozens of other stories in newspapers across the country, and that's what happened.

National stories about the VONGO launch generated nearly 300 million news media impressions in a 10-day period, driving Web site traffic and consumer subscriptions. The new offering from Starz earned the status as one of the "buzz products to watch in 2006."

The communications people who specialize in this kind of media relations get the respect of their companies, clients and journalists alike. What they accomplish is earned media, which builds valuable image awareness and credibility.

There have long been lines of separation between earned and paid media ... until recently. Today some enterprising, generally smaller, newspapers and online journalistic outfits have turned to selling so-called news coverage. I guess the rationale is that when they are struggling for income, journalistic ethics can be compromised or ignored completely. As a result, the traditional lines of separation between advertising and news have at times gotten blurry.

A department store in a shopping mall wants recognition for writing a check and getting involved in worthwhile local community events. They want a photo of their general manager shaking hands with local civic leaders, and they want a story that quotes them saying self-congratulatory things that — they hope — will make them look like they are giving back to the town in which they do business.

A news story? Hardly! It's self-serving fluff that most editors would ignore. In fact if you push most responsible editors too hard on the subject, it will come back and hurt you when you do have legitimate news.

Yet a growing number of generally smaller newspapers — squeezed by shrinking traditional advertising revenues — will sell space, usually on a special page in the paper, where businesses can run self-promotional pieces that they hope readers will think is news. News? Who are they kidding? It's advertising, and readers can smell it across the room. And the paper wonders why their readers develop the perception that they are nothing more than an advertising rag.

I'm always a little baffled when I hear of such practices, because it would be so much more credible and effective for a business to invest those same dollars to work with a professional public relations person and come up with a legitimate news angle that will result in a good story in the media. That's earned media coverage — the good stuff.

Perception Is the Highest Form of Reality

Perception is the most powerful force in communications. We make decisions based on how we perceive something or someone. And no two perceptions are exactly alike. You and I can be poles apart in our perception of something, and both be "right," because our perceptions define our reality.

During our individual life journeys, we each have endless learning experiences and challenges that influence our perceptions.

You and I see a cloud. It reminds you of the Wyeth painting of a giant with a club; to me, it looks like rain coming. Two different perceptions, both correct.

The dictionary defines *perception* as "intuitive recognition of a truth." In fact perception is far more complex, intangible and fragile than that.

When jockeying to capture audience awareness, too many companies look for a basic truth — or reality — in hopes it will set their organization apart from others: "we're the *leading* ..." or "the *largest* ..."

Unfortunately this strategy lumps them into an enormous universe of other organizations saying the same thing. It's a boast that won't cut through competitive clutter. Journalists and savvy news consumers alike are alert to and suspicious of the overuse of superlatives, especially when the declarations are not backed up by a compelling track record. The overuse of self-aggrandizing adjectives was a popular style, especially by technology companies during the tech boom of the late 90s, yet it often demotes potential for authentic credibility today.

The conscious and subconscious factors that influence perception have been debated for centuries by academics and philosophers — and more recently, and from a less skilled perspective, by communications professionals. And still your perception of something tomorrow might be different than it is today and changed today from what it was yesterday. That's human nature and the nature of perceptions. We perceive events, people, companies, products and things in different ways, and we each are motivated by our individual perceptions.

Not surprisingly, understanding perception is critically important in practicing media relations today. We want to, of course, strive for accuracy and clarity in what we tell the media, reducing chances for confusion and misperceptions. We may both be right when we see different things in the cloud, but in media and public relations, the perception that counts is that of the media.

Here's an example: If you have a policy that all comments to the media need to be cleared by an attorney, then you could be building a perception with reporters of being defensive, that you've got something to hide.

The same is true if you read from a prepared statement in response to routine questions from reporters. Whether you read accurately, you are sending a signal of defensiveness. If your organization is already in hot water, you don't want to exacerbate the situation by acting evasive.

Here are six things a company, individual or organization can do to change perception:

- *Get outside yourself.* Look at your image challenge from the perspective of an outsider, such as a client or customer or investor or the media. Understand how others see you.

- *Walk into the future.* Define how you want your organization to be described two or three years from now by people who are important to your company.

- *Challenge conventional thinking.* Just because it seemingly felt good a couple of years ago doesn't mean it will work in today's highly competitive arenas. It's OK — in fact, necessary — to discard bad habits in media relations and try new approaches.

- *Avoid "committee speak."* Defining your organization by committee often results in too many words that say too little, too vaguely.

- *Steer away from overused 50-cent marketing words.* You know what they are: the dull adjectives pulled off the shelf when we can't think of anything else. Words like *unique, innovative* and *leading provider* have been overworked to the point of becoming meaningless.

- *Be consistent.* Once you have decided what to say and how to say it, stick with that consistent approach in working with the news media. Consistency works to build trust and helps to overcome confusion that can adversely influence an otherwise good perception.

In media relations it doesn't matter whether you are the "largest" or the "best." If you are perceived as an organization that is communicating openly, candidly and clearly, then you are sending positive signals to your audiences, including the news media. It helps you to be perceived as a winner.

Nothing Is Secret

In today's world of e-mail, the Internet and instant messaging, it's folly to think that anything is secret. Documents, notes from meetings, anything — regardless of the level of confidentiality — can be sent across town or around the world in a flash, with a single click of a mouse. It happens all the time.

A friend told me that supposedly private e-mails he had exchanged with a business contact at the U.S. Department of Agriculture or USDA popped up unexpectedly and publicly in a Yahoo search of his name several weeks later. He understandably was shocked to see his e-mails so publicly available. The episode was blamed on an Internet server security glitch at USDA.

In media relations, the moment you sit down to write any document — whether a news release or strategic plan or e-mail — it's important to keep in mind that whatever you draft could become public, even inadvertently. Nothing is secret.

Throughout this book, I have stressed the importance of truthfulness and transparency in getting your story out and working with the news media. As I wrote earlier, communications with the news media mirrors behavior. An organization that dodges facts and manipulates issues will ultimately erode whatever credibility it may have.

What happened at the Washington, D.C., zoo is classic.

Under Dr. Lucy Spelman's watch as director of the National Zoo in Washington, nearly two dozen animals died, including some rare and endangered species. Some veterinary records were changed after the fact. In one case a popular elephant died at an early age of tuberculosis for lack of an easily obtainable vaccination. In another case two rare zebras died from hypothermia and malnutrition. It all came to light through a series of reports in *The Washington Post*.

How did the *Post* know? Somebody talked. A front-page story by Henri E. Cauvin had all the grisly details:

"In a confidential strategy paper produced by Hill & Knowlton, the zoo is urged to be open with the media but aggressive in containing any fallout from the deaths. The 23-page plan warns that continuing inquiries by *The Washington Post* could emerge as a story of national import, creating a crisis that would imperil the zoo's bid for full accreditation and threaten the job of Director Lucy H. Spelman.

"Lucy Spelman's credibility as a leader may appear to be diminished, with possible requests for her removal," Hill & Knowlton, the public relations agency, said in a list of potential scenarios that could follow more "negative news stories" on the zoo.

What happened was that Spelman paid the PR firm $50,000 of the zoo's money to try to clean up her image, but it backfired. Her scheme became front-page news. It created a perception that good PR was more important than taking responsible and affirmative steps to ensure the safe welfare of zoo animals. Zoo employees were outraged by her behavior, and confidential documents got into the hands of a reporter. The resulting series of stories portrayed Spelman as an inept zoo director and Hill & Knowlton as more concerned about her reputation than that of the zoo.

It didn't stop there. The arrogance of the zoo's leader resulted in a *Washington Post* editorial that began this way: "If only the animals could talk, we might learn more troubling truths about their care and feeding at the National Zoo. Incomplete or altered veterinary records have obscured instances of apparent neglect, misdiagnosis and other serious mistakes in connection with the deaths of at least 23 animals."

News is leaked to the media every day when unusual things happen. For example, in a rare peek behind the curtains of the Wal-Mart retail empire, *The New York Times* carried a front-page story about remarks made by the company's chief executive H. Lee Scott on a private, internal company Web site. A manager had asked him why the "largest company on the planet cannot offer some type of medical benefits." Scott, apparently annoyed, responded by accusing the manager of disloyalty and suggested he quit.

The exchange became public when copies of Scott's postings covering two years — two years! — were given to the *Times* by a group backed by unions and others pressing Wal-Mart to improve its employee wages and benefits.

Nothing — absolutely nothing — can be kept secret. The more egregious the sin, the more likely it will make it to the media. Remember the infamous Deep Throat of Nixon's Watergate, the Pentagon papers that a courageous Daniel Ellsberg released to *The New York Times* and all the exposed cover-ups? That was over 30 years ago, long before e-mail, blogs, the Internet and a 24-hour news cycle. Secrecy is much harder today.

Although you can't expect anything to be secret forever, you can maximize your chances of confidentiality and minimize your chances of damaging your reputation. Here are some tips on handling information before it gets public:

- *Label a draft as a draft.* When writing a document, such as a news release and media briefing document, type DRAFT at the top of the first page. Include the draft version number, date and your own initials. Then, if the document becomes public prematurely, your organization has a legitimate defense that the document was a draft, not a final statement.

- *Avoid e-mailing everyone.* It's a bad habit at many organizations to include extraneous people on e-mails. Limit e-mail daisy chains. Especially on issues of your organization's image and reputation, only share e-mails and documents between people who are relevant to the topic.

- *Have signed confidentiality statements.* Employees will often think twice before leaking sensitive material when they've signed a confidentiality statement that clearly spells out that termination may result from intentionally telling secrets.

Of course, if you've invested the time to develop personal relationships with the reporters who cover your organization, that's the best safeguard in handling leaks. You will have developed credibility with the news media that will no doubt eclipse that of the informant.

There's nothing better in a potentially hostile media environment than to be on a first-name basis with key reporters. Having an established and trusted professional relationship with the news media can work to turn around wrong impressions, correct misinformation, help defuse a possibly unfavorable story, and provide a better and more accurate perspective for journalists.

There Is No Such Thing as "No Comment"

If you are facing some tough issues that you will be asked about by the media, and you want to shout, "No comment," why not just hold up a big red sign that says "Guilty!" The end result would be about the same. It is simply irresponsible for a spokesperson to say "no comment," because it will usually result in more damage.

Luladey Tadesse, a reporter at the Wilmington, Delaware, *News Journal*, told me that "no comment" is really a comment. "It makes you look defensive," she said. She is so correct.

To a professional journalist, "no comment" can be a telltale sign of a bigger problem.

During 30 years as a journalist and strategic communications consultant, I can't tell you the number of times I've seen bad situations get worse because a spokesperson decided to say — usually in a curt tone of voice — "no comment" to the media rather than find a better response.

"No comment" immediately creates a feeling of fear and mistrust about an individual or organization, regardless of the circumstances.

It usually happens because some attorney mandates that the company say nothing but "no comment." It's irresponsible and shows disregard for an organization's brand and reputation.

"The worst type of public relations person, usually found in-house at some organization, is the one who refuses to comment," said Jon Ashworth of *The Times* in London.

"No comment" suggests guilt, arrogance and abruptness — all the emotional elements you want to avoid during a supercharged situation.

It implies you have something to hide. Whatever the level of desperation, frustration and aggravation when things go bad, those two words are never an option.

Here is an alternative approach to handling a potentially damaging situation for your organization:

First, when the phone rings and it's a reporter calling you, remember that there is no law that says you must talk with the reporter at that moment. If you feel unprepared or ambushed, buy some time to collect your thoughts and think of something to say. Explain to the reporter that you are more than happy to speak with him or her, but you are in the middle of something. Ask if he or she is on deadline and negotiate a reasonable time frame to return the call, such as a half hour to one hour.

Next — and this is essential — ask the reporter to give you an idea of what he or she wants to talk about. Never ask reporters what questions they are going to ask; just query the subject matter. Most reporters will work with you. Then get together with your public relations people and others to formulate a meaningful statement other than "no comment." Buying some time is an invaluable tool in media relations, because it allows you to get over being nervous about talking with a reporter, possibly over an adverse issue, and helps you to focus. Finally — and this is really important — contact the reporter as promised.

If your organization is facing an unfavorable situation that might draw media questions, it is essential to work in advance of any media contact and develop a response or statement, no matter how brief it might be. Think of it as a good opportunity to turn around a negative perception. A possible response could begin something like this: "While we are not prepared to make a formal statement at this time ..." and then bridge to one or two brief messages about the situation that you believe are important. In that way you are giving the impression of being responsive, responsible and accountable.

Lastly, remember that it's OK to be brief. In fact the fewer words the better as long as they are not "no comment." The media will live with a response that's only a sentence or two because you are taking the time to at least say *something* during a difficult time. Consider a response that might elicit sympathy: "While this is a challenging time, we wanted to say ..." and again bridge to a brief message.

A bridge *is an interview tactic to control and redirect an interview back to the subject that you want to talk about, using the salient messages that you have developed and rehearsed in advance.*

Whether you feel it or not, show genuine sincerity and a willingness to communicate. A positive attitude often will communicate as much as actual words. It may be your only constructive option.

If faced with a developing, possibly negative situation, why not say, "We want to be clear and accurate in anything we say. We are still gathering information that we will share with you when we have the whole picture."

In other words, there are many statements you can make to the news media other than "no comment." Those two words are not an option. View an adverse situation as an opportunity to briefly deliver positive messages that communicate responsiveness and concern.

Off-the-Record Versus Background

The first thing to remember is that there is really no such thing as an "off-the-record" comment, particularly if you want to maintain some level of credibility. And unless you are employed by the White House or the National Security Agency, there's really no reason to talk off the record.

From my interviews with journalists for this book, the majority opinion is that off-the-record comments can get too complicated and too fraught with hazards, particularly when all a reporter is seeking is a story. Strictly speaking, *off the record* means that nothing you have to say can be reported by a journalist. Nothing. So, in that context there is no reason to be having the conversation.

Nevertheless I have seen occasions when less experienced newsmakers — often corporate executives — have suddenly proclaimed during an interview, "Now, off the record, let me say ..." The only reason for the statement was, perhaps, to create a faux sense of gravitas or drama over an otherwise routine interview. But this disclaimer can be bewildering to a reporter, particularly if it's not in the logical flow of the interview subject or there is no purpose for it other than to create a false level of importance.

If you have something to share with the news media, there is seldom anything to be gained by attempting to speak off the record with a reporter. I know many journalists who will smartly refuse to allow interviewees to go off the record during an interview. When you talk off the record, integrity can be compromised, and enduring trust in a relationship with the media can be put to the test. The best advice is to avoid any off-the-record situation.

On the other hand background briefings without attribution to a specific source have become commonplace, particularly in political and government circles. Background briefings are a valuable tool in media relations today. We hear and read all the time statements that begin with phrases like "According to White House sources …" or "Military commanders say …"

Background briefings are helpful to the news media to provide perspective and depth of understanding about an issue, event or story. A reliable source provides information, yet the name of the source really isn't important to the story.

A word of caution: Background briefings with the news media can be fraught with hazards. Anything you say in a background briefing can be reported, so there must be additional ground rules clearly agreed upon in advance. For example, in the background briefing, the name of your organization could be used unless you specify otherwise. Another risk is that you might forget to ask reporters not to use your name or job title.

If you have told a reporter that you will provide background without attribution, then whatever you say can be reported, but your name will not be used. If you forget to set the boundaries, then anything is fair game.

The Value of an Apology

I have never failed to be impressed by how a simple, honest apology can defuse the most volatile situation, often averting a communications crisis for a corporation or politician.

In another time, in the cowboy film *She Wore a Yellow Ribbon*, John Wayne growled "never apologize, and never explain." But that was then, over 50 years ago in a macho western. This is now. Today apologies can do wonders.

Consider this example: "Gov. John Rowland changed his story Friday and acknowledged that friends — including some under suspicion in a federal corruption investigation — paid for work on his summer home," reported Susan Haigh of The Associated Press. "Rowland's admission, made public in a statement came ten days after he insisted he alone had paid for improvements on the house at Bantam Lake."

Another politician confirms what we believe about most politicians: that they accept payoffs. Yet in this case, Rowland exacerbates his situation by lying and then changing his story and announcing it in a written statement. A statement! Who's going to believe a written statement? Why not just come clean and stand up in front of the microphones and reporters with notebooks and say something that begins with "I've made a terrible mistake. I apologize, and I'm going to do everything possible to make it right ..."

Rowland was later found guilty and went to prison.

Equally astonishing is the absolute refusal by some organizations and titans of industry to ever admit to any mistakes, even when their hands are caught in the cookie jar. In fact it seems that the larger the scope of misdoings and egregious misconduct, the more likely that arrogance will prevent the perpetrators from even considering the value of an apology.

It must be something in the American ethos that a guy who makes an apology is some sort of "girlie man," to borrow Arnold Schwarzenegger's words. Attorneys advise clients to shun the actual word *apology* in favor of *regret*.

Did you ever hear an apology from Enron, Global Crossing or Worldcom? Nope. The message we heard was one of blame and excuses, seemingly driven by greed and arrogance. We were left with the impression that many of those titans of business were just well-compensated crooks.

Another example: Hurricane Isabel cut a destructive swath up the east coast of the United States, leaving hundreds of thousands of people with no power for days. Several of the power companies were slow to restore service. It was disclosed in the media that they had cut back the number of repair crews needed to upgrade power lines in order to show a better bottom line to investors.

Rather than standing up in a news conference and saying simply, "We made a mistake. We apologize, and we are now working feverishly to restore electricity to your homes," the power-company executives attempted to defend their decisions. They did battle with the news media. They made the media their enemy rather than saying they screwed up. It was classic John Wayne behavior, circa 1950. Yet today such behavior comes off as incompetence and appears to emphasize greed over a clear focus on customer service. It wasn't smart, and the companies were broiled by the public, the media, the politicians and … the investors.

There are unfortunately far too many executives and attorneys who choose to duke it out (pun intended) with tough stances. The worse the situation, the greater the arrogance — and often the greater the media feast of one story after another. Denying responsibility or twisting facts, especially in the face of evidence to the contrary, will actually create a news story. Hey, just apologize, make amends and move forward.

President George W. Bush managed to reduce damage to the reputation of his administration by accepting responsibility, albeit belatedly, for incompetence by the Federal Emergency Management Administration in responding to Hurricane Katrina in 2005. A week after the hurricane, people were still dying along the Gulf Coast, and the region was in chaos, because no aid had arrived from the federal government.

When it was apparent that the government had no plan, and the administration was being scalded by everyone from the media to both Republicans and Democrats, Mr. Bush essentially said, "We were wrong, we made mistakes, but here's what we are doing now ..." and outlined a plan for assistance. Sadly, though, his apology was not subsequently linked to concrete actions and timely relief for those whose lives were devastated by the hurricane, giving rise to what some Bush administration observers called Bush's "smirk factor," a habit of making an apology or statement that is, in reality, neither sincere nor backed up by action.

Connecticut-based communications strategist Jane Genova counsels organizations on the value of creating goodwill through an apology. She said nonapologizers might be smart to explore using mea culpa as a power tool, and she shared these examples from her work:

1. *Just observe.* When anyone makes a sincere apology, we listen. "I landed an assignment in the mega competitive hospitality industry by recognizing that even the most unhappy guest will be turned around by an authentic and detailed apology," she said.

2. *Give up on the "cult of the self."* Did the inward, self-focus theory ever work? That's questionable. In an interconnected, volatile global economy, who can go it alone? That's why the Eastern philosophy of "no-self" is catching on rapidly. If we aren't defending the self, apology comes naturally.

3. *Decide if we want to be right/appear to be right or be successful.* Surrendering on this one is the necessary inner paradigm shift that makes apology possible.

4. *Ignore the lawyers, initially.* We can apologize in ways that won't invite legal action or strengthen the case of the opposition. After we make a decision to do a mea culpa, then we should listen to the lawyers.

5. *Try out apologizing.* When we get the favorable attention of others out there, we know we're doing it right.

When talk show host Oprah Winfrey realized she had been duped by one of her chosen authors, James Frey, she accused him on live television of lying about the supposed facts in his book *A Million Little Pieces*, and she apologized to her audience for originally endorsing the book. The high-profile celebrity knew the power of an apology; done right, it can be disarming.

Unquestionably a sincere apology has become an effective tool in communications and media relations. Most everyone will give a break or second chance to someone who admits a mistake.

We are human. We do our best. We are not perfect. We make honest mistakes. In extremely difficult times, an apology can be an effective and proven method of controlling media relations.

A Gas-Station Mentality

Journalists who cover the high-technology industry have told me how often they note the lack of creativity by companies — from multinational giants to tiny startups — in describing new products and services. As a result, high-tech hopefuls often miss opportunities to capture all-important competitive differentiation.

This is a true story: The marketing communications staff at a software company was stumped, trying to figure out how to describe a new product that was being rushed to market after a competitor beat them to the punch. What could they say to capture the media's attention about their product? How could they create clever positioning? Words failed. But that wasn't all that failed.

Their boss got a brilliant idea: He instructed his staff to check the competitor's Web site and see how they had described their new product and then ... kinda, sorta ... plagiarize that description. Sound familiar? Unfortunately it's all too familiar in the technology industry. And it's a recipe for more failure. It's a strategy for landing yourself in second place ... or worse.

Everyone — the financial markets, investors, venture capitalists and all of us ordinary people — likes technology because it's exciting, and it makes our lives easier and more manageable. When a company with substance comes along, technology can be a fun investment. And yet the high-technology world, with few exceptions, is too often a vast wasteland of blandness when it comes to distinctive and imaginative marketing communications and media relations.

No one is certain why, but technology has traditionally been wrapped up in talking about itself, using words that may sound impressive but mean little or nothing — "technobabble," as one reporter called it.

Take a closer look at all the failed technological pioneers and, with few exceptions, you will find companies that pretty much used the same words and jargon to say the same things, regardless of their product or service. How many times have you heard phrases like "the world's leading innovative integrated systems solutions provider ..."

It's a lot like gas stations: When one gas station opens at an intersection, others follow, promoting themselves in the same way, saying the same thing. It's all copycat. Same with technology: When one tech company promotes itself with tired and overused 50-cent marketing words, others copy. The rest of us, seeing nothing authentic, get bored and lose interest.

In media relations, when we get lazy and copy what a competitor is doing, we forfeit any chance to gain an edge and win. We lose any chance at competitive differentiation.

Nowhere is it more prevalent than in the information technology or IT sector. It seems like everyone is an IT company, from business consultants to software companies to financial institutions and your local newspaper. It's a catch-all phrase for companies that can't figure out how to explain what they do. Remember the 1980s habit of stores calling themselves such things as "Kitchenware ... *and More*"? Recently it's been "IT and More."

But despite all of this, technology not only holds the promise for America's success and security, it also has the opportunity to be an enduring darling of Wall Street. So here's an easy four-step checklist to help you authentically trumpet the true value of your enterprise and separate the leaders from the losers:

- *Think and talk outside of yourself.* Most of the time the news media and your primary audiences would prefer to hear about the value of what your organization does, rather than hear adjective-filled pronouncements about your company. Invest the time in some high-level strategic thinking to define how you want your company to be perceived and talked about in two or three years. That strategy will help to guide a positive brand-building marketing communications approach today and into the future.

- *Make that strategic vision come alive.* Develop an original, practical and working strategic plan that uses clever tactics to gain attention to credibly and realistically achieve what's called *competitive positioning.* Remember, it doesn't really matter that much whether you are the "largest" or "best" organization. If you are viewed as a leader, then you've won.

- *Stand in the shoes of your clients or audiences.* Learn how to communicate the benefit of your product or service to the person who ultimately makes the decision and has the authority to buy.

- *Talk in sound bites, not elevator speeches.* A sound bite is to describe your endeavor, precisely, in one breath — about 16 seconds — using words that are understandable, credible, exciting and memorable. An *elevator speech*, although popular, takes too long — particularly if you are headed for the 44th floor. Reporters, distracted by others who can say it concisely, will lose interest.

- *Avoid jargon, acronyms, buzzwords and trendy clichés.* Few phrases lead to more communication confusion and misunderstandings than the prefabricated and empty clichés of business, such as *value proposition, actionable, learning partners, maximizing, critical path* and *visioning.* It's a long list of ambiguous words to be wary of. They can impede clear communication.

When used properly, these principles of effective communications work not just for technology companies, but also for any organization. Straight-shooting media relations requires clear and precise differentiation so that the media and audiences know you from your competitor.

The challenge is to overcome a common thread among most companies: the inability to incisively and concisely describe their individual value and what's genuinely special about what they deliver to their audiences, their customers. Too often the company stalls in its own words and business-school jargon.

When technology and other industry sectors occasionally run out of gas — and they can — it's your job to fill up their tanks with high-octane creativity. Throw in a wash and wax, and get back out on the racetrack with timely and compelling communications with journalists that makes positive news for your organization.

Hiding Behind Paper

Perhaps one of the most common "sins" of public relations and communications people is never actually doing the work to identify how to bridge the gap between what is *newsworthy* for the media and the promotional message you are pushing on behalf of a client or employer.

Consequently too many, if not most, media campaigns are centered around — maybe it's more accurate to say hidden behind — a systematic flood of news releases and expensive media materials that are sent out carpet-bomb style to the media, most often to the wrong people.

It happens hundreds of times each day: An organization issues a news release via a paid news release wire service, such as PR Newswire or BusinessWire, or through a service that bulk e-mails thousands of news contacts, and those e-mails are often caught in spam filters and never seen. Somehow there is a feeling that if the news industry is smothered by a release, someone might pay attention. On the contrary, such mass distribution is an unproductive way of getting the attention of today's news media — and about as effective as dropping thousands of copies of the release from an airplane, except that the latter might actually get some news coverage ... albeit not so positive, I suspect.

Out of fairness, such methods to distribute financial news announcements — for example earnings reports and news of market and shareholder interest — provide an efficient way to meet disclosure requirements.

But the paid news-distribution services today are also clogged with so many other poorly focused and irrelevant news releases that journalists tell me they tend to ignore many, if not most, of the releases because they just do not have the time to sort through all of them.

If there is one common trait among many people who are charged with media relations, it is a reluctance to actually interface on any personal level with the news media in any way, such as through a phone call. Odd as it might seem, too many public relations people hide behind news releases, media lists, mailings, bulk e-mails and faxes. They avoid actually picking up the phone to speak with a journalist and develop a working relationship.

Organizations spend fortunes on so-called news-distribution services to get their news releases and media materials in front of as many journalists as possible, seemingly to help them avoid having to go to the trouble of picking up a phone and making a personal pitch to a reporter.

It's fairly common to hear PR agency executives tell their clients that an "exclusive" news service was used to get their release before several thousand reporters, as if to suggest that the PR people have somehow managed to stop the presses and gotten the attention of hordes of reporters to read their client's news announcement. Such claims can only be labeled as "murky truth." While a news distribution service might have the capability to send a news release to thousands of journalists via e-mail, there's no guarantee that anyone will actually really read it or even consider doing a story, much less the release ever resulting in a story.

Today an increasing number of media relations professionals are turning to newer and alternative approaches to produce meaningful results. These new approaches do not require sending out hundreds of news releases. The process begins by crafting a legitimate news story, then focusing on only that handful of journalists who cover an organization. The technique is to build trusted relationships with journalists, provide incisive information, and set the stage to work with those journalists to develop a relevant and timely news story. That's the way to maximize control of your story and improve the chance it will come out the way you hoped.

"Don't overwhelm the assignment desk and producers with too much information," counsels C-SPAN's Steve Scully. "With all the paperwork we deal with everyday, less is better. Accurate and *timely* is required."

"With all the paperwork we deal with everyday, less is better. Accurate and *timely* is required." — Steve Scully, producer, C-SPAN

The traditional wisdom among PR people that "more is better" is both ineffective in contemporary media relations and often annoying to journalists. Effective media relations today mandates approaching the right journalist with the right story angle at the right time. It requires making a personal contact rather than hiding behind paper.

A general manager of a public radio station tells friends she has built a terrific library at home with all the books sent to her over the years by book publicists who never took the time to make a phone call and figure out who to send a book to in order to schedule an interview on the air for the author. She got on the publicity mailing list and received a ton of books. By the way, the general manager or station manager is never the right person to contact.

On that subject, certainly many public and news/talk radio stations are interested in interviewing authors about new books on timely issues, but you will find that each program has a producer designated to review and consider possible interviews. It's the responsibility of a public relations person to find those stations in respective markets, identify which programs to approach and make an initial phone call to the right producer to ask how they prefer to be pitched about a possible interview. You will find they all have individual styles and preferences and that a phone call is a valuable first step toward developing what can be a lasting relationship.

In a TV newsroom in Denver, they still remember the time when a local law firm representing billionaire Philip Anschutz faxed in a 17-page news release about 30 minutes before airtime for the early evening newscast. The fax cover page demanded that the news release be read

... verbatim. Not surprisingly the newscast producer ignored the entire news release. A heated exchange later erupted between the news producer and one of the attorneys after the attorney called demanding an explanation of why the release wasn't mentioned on the air.

Jon Ashworth, business features editor at *The Times* of London, said, "I am constantly being 'pitched' with ideas for soft articles that are often just glorified ads. The PR agencies are putting in the calls so that they can tick names off a list — part of justifying their fee. I find this a waste of everyone's time. Overall, most journalists see PR people as a necessary evil."

PR representatives as a general rule are aggressive in cranking out news releases and dutifully sending a blizzard of them out to as many journalists as possible. Yet they rarely make any sort of personal follow-up contact with the media or are responsive if — holy smokes! — a reporter actually calls for more information if the news release catches their eye.

That's particularly the style of PR people in the book or tourism promotion business. They send out paper or e-mail news releases to massive, generalized and seldom-updated media lists, then apparently go to lunch. Countless reporters have complained that the ball is dropped at that point.

A major national PR agency, for example, supposedly represents a venerable old resort in the western mountains of Virginia and blindly sends out news releases. But when reporters call the agency about a possible story, they always get the voice mail of the PR person assigned to the account, and messages left are not returned.

Reporters say that book publicists are also among the more lethargic. The publicists send review copies of books with news releases neatly tucked inside the front cover to seemingly every journalist on the planet. But call one of the publicists back to ask for a photo of the author to be e-mailed to you or to ask that a chapter excerpt be sent, and you might as well be talking to a brick wall. Their approach to media relations seems to center on mailing books and news releases to a media list that's apparently been around for years and then go to lunch.

A friend at *USA Today* told me that the book reviewers, alone, at his newspaper receive over 3,500 books each month from authors and publishers looking for publicity. Only a handful of them are ever actually reviewed.

Walk into the newsroom of any daily newspaper or television station when the mail arrives, and you will be amazed at the volume of unsolicited paper — news releases, media kits and boxes of promotional stuff — that shows up.

At *USA Today*, for example, where editors are required to read, however briefly, everything that comes in, the mailroom guys cart it in, using wheeled garbage cans that are piled high with paper. It's a conga line of garbage cans. Some of the mail is addressed merely to "Occupant, Newsroom," and that's usually the first to be pitched in the trash. The staff makes jokes about it being recycled into fireplace logs.

The most common PR practice is to send news releases to the wrong news organization, akin to sending a release on gardening tips to *Aviation Week & Space Technology*. Here's the lead of an actual release that was sent to an online magazine for baby boomers. The release had no relevance to baby boomers or seemingly anything else:

ERC DATAPLUS INTRODUCES SELECTECH® 6.0 INTE-GRATED ATS AND INTERVIEWER TRAINING AT HR EXECUTIVE'S HR TECHNOLOGY CONFERENCE & EXPO

Comprehensive Applicant Tracking Solution Uniquely Integrates Hourly and Management Applicants on a Single Platform Online elearning System Creates Better Interviewers and Better Interviews

Norwalk, CT — October 11, 2005 — ERC Dataplus, Inc., a leading Human Resource technology company, today announced the release of Selectech® 6.0 Integrated ATS and Selectech® Interviewer Training at HR Executive's HR Technology Conference & Expo held in Chicago's McCormick Place. "Selectech 6.0 takes applicant management to a new level," said ERC Dataplus CEO Paul Rathblott. "By providing a single platform that integrates pre-qualification, screening, validated assessment and on-boarding for hourly and management applicants, Selectech 6.0 provides HR executives an unprecedented ability to streamline processes and significantly enhance the effectiveness of their applicant management activities."

Mind-boggling industry jargon aside, this release has an 18-word headline plus a 22-word subhead, making it among the longest headline combination I have ever seen and also longer than some *USA Today* stories. Despite the headline's length, it says essentially nothing.

In fairness much of the unsolicited news material sent to news organizations is addressed to the "Editor" or someone by name. But too often media materials are addressed to someone who moved to another news outfit — or in some cases — to someone who died years ago.

Typical news media materials begin with a form-type generic cover letter that explains the critical importance of the news from the sender's perspective. The letters generally have an urgent stop-the-presses tone about them and suggest that this news is the greatest announcement since Al Gore supposedly invented the Internet. More often than not the cover letter fails to suggest how this so-called news might actually be made into a news story. Sadly for the hopeful writer, these news materials are pushed aside by items that carry a more genuine tone or are more professionally presented.

Most journalists prefer a specific, personalized story pitch rather than a news release. So many newspeople have said they need "an idea that is news-driven" rather than a typical fluffy news release.

"Give me numbers, think of other possible sources and even give sources who might be on the other side. That is really helpful. What is the controversial point, who might we want to talk to on the other side," said a wire-service reporter.

Pat Piper produced "The Larry King Show" for over a decade on Mutual Radio and today collaborates with King on a variety of books.

He thinks most PR people oversell to the media and compulsively send too much "stuff."

"Here's a newsflash," Piper said. "The world may revolve around your client but the world I deal with doesn't usually include your client or cause. I always have a trash can when I open the mail. I always have a delete button when I read an e-mail attachment."

> "The world may revolve around your client but the world I deal with doesn't usually include your client or cause. I always have a trash can when I open the mail. I always have a delete button when I read an e-mail attachment." — Pat Piper, news producer and journalist

Denver-based newspaper columnist and former ABC Network News correspondent Greg Dobbs gives this useful advice: "Ask yourself what the media wants and needs. The answer won't necessarily be the message you want to communicate, but if you don't get them 'in the door,' the strongest message on earth will have no impact.

"How do you figure out what the media wants and needs? Simple: pretend you are a reporter, and your only stake in the matter is in getting a good story, not in getting your message out. In other words, put yourself in the reporter's shoes and offer what he or she is looking for. In short, get their attention, then work on carving that message."

> "How do you figure out what the media wants and needs? Put yourself in the reporter's shoes and offer what he or she is looking for." — Greg Dobbs, broadcaster and former ABC Network News correspondent

Media relations is not blitzing everyone in the newsroom with the same news release or media kit. It all comes down to establishing a relationship — making a phone call to the news organization, identifying the right reporter, developing a credible and balanced news pitch, and delivering that pitch in the brief and incisive manner that reporters prefer.

A Time to Question Bad Habits

This chapter is about a misguided trend by some corporations and organizations — call it a bad habit — of using news releases and other materials under the guise of working with the news media to actually manipulate credibility. It's about *safe-harbor* statements, which are tantamount to saying "nothing you are about to read is true," and *about* statements, which are blatant self-promotion. Both adversely impact credibility in dealing with the news media.

The idea of including in news releases a piece of legal language called a safe-harbor statement gained popularity in the mid-1990s with high-technology companies. Their attorneys believed the companies needed protection from themselves and from many of the often-outlandish claims they made in news releases and other promotional materials. In other words their own attorneys questioned whether the bravado of tech companies was truthful.

So the attorneys came up with standard safe-harbor language, or boilerplate, to be included at the end of every news release, that they hoped would legally protect a company from being accused of outright lying. Here's an example of a safe-harbor statement from a technology company:

> This press release may include statements that may constitute "forward-looking statements," including its estimates of future business prospects or financial results and statements containing the words "believe," "estimate," "project," "expect" or similar expressions. Forward-looking statements inherently involve risks and uncertainties that could cause actual results of this company and its subsidiaries (collectively, the "Company") to differ materially from the forward-looking statements. Factors that could contribute to such

differences include: the ability of the Company to implement and achieve widespread customer acceptance of its Report Services software on a timely basis; the Company's ability to recognize deferred revenue through delivery of products or satisfactory performance of services; continued acceptance of the Company's products in the marketplace; the timing of significant orders; delays in the Company's ability to develop or ship new products; market acceptance of new products; competitive factors; general economic conditions; currency fluctuations; and other risks detailed in the Company's registration statements and periodic reports filed with the Securities and Exchange Commission. By making these forward-looking statements, the Company undertakes no obligation to update these statements for revisions or changes after the date of this release.

In 186 words, or about 20 percent of the total content of the news release, the company warns, "Reader, beware!" It's a classic cover-your-butt approach. A journalist takes one look and understandably wonders whether anything in the news release is true.

And then there are the about statements, like mini-advertisements within news releases. Here's one that appears in news releases from the insurance company MassMutual:

> MassMutual Financial Group comprised of member companies with more than $370 billion in assets under management as of June 30, 2005 is a global, growth-oriented, diversified financial services organization providing life insurance, annuities, disability income insurance, long-term care insurance, retirement planning products, structured settlement annuities, trust services, money management, and other financial products and services.
> The MassMutual Financial Group is a marketing designation (or fleet name) for Massachusetts Mutual Life Insurance Company (MassMutual) and its affiliates, which include: Oppenheimer-Funds, Inc.; Babson Capital Management LLC; Baring Asset Management Limited; Cornerstone Real Estate Advisers LLC; MML Investors Services, Inc.; The MassMutual Trust Company, FSB; MML Bay State Life Insurance Company, C.M. Life Insurance Company, and MassMutual International, Inc.

*Securities offered by registered representatives of MML Investors Services, Inc., 1414 Main Street, Springfield, MA 01144-1013 (413) 737-8400.
You can't predict. You can prepare.® is a registered trademark of MassMutual.

Good grief! Nothing in that or most other about statements has any relevance or timeliness in news releases. Yet, over the objections of many in the news business, about statements have become common in many news releases. They are generally lengthy, distracting and boastful boilerplate describing great things about the company or organization. It's self-serving ego fluff that impresses few people and certainly few journalists.

Here's the about statement from a company you might think should be more savvy, PeopleSoft:

PeopleSoft (Nasdaq: PSFT) is the world's leading provider of application software for the real-time enterprise. PeopleSoft pure Internet software enables organizations to reduce costs and increase productivity by directly connecting customers, suppliers, partners and employees to business processes on-line, in real time. PeopleSoft's integrated, best-in-class applications include Customer Relationship Management, Supply Chain Management, Human Capital Management, Financial Management and Application Integration. Today more than 5,200 organizations in 140 countries run on PeopleSoft software.

Ask reporters what they think of about statements, as I have, and they will tell you that it's usually common information easily found with a couple of clicks on the organization's Web site.

In fact a survey of journalists by TEKgroup International, an online PR resource company, showed that a majority of reporters said that online newsrooms is their preferred method of gathering information about an organization for stories.

The simpler an online newsroom is to navigate and the more tools and information you offer to reporters in one location, the easier it becomes for reporters to write about your organization. That translates into increased coverage.

There is, however, a significant gap between what journalists expect to find on corporate Web sites and what PR practitioners actually provide. For starters reporters complain that while many sites archive news releases, just as many still do not offer adequate contact information.

Today's savvy media relations professionals can make everything easily available online, including media kits, corporate backgrounders, fact sheets about services or products, industry white papers, photos and visuals, case studies and even bylined feature stories. Yet some old corporate habits are hard to break.

The about statement at the end of each news release from J. C. Penney headquarters in Plano, Texas, is typical of so many organizations and appears to simply be an advertisement for the company. The subject of this news release was to announce National Football League wristbands for the J. C. Penney Afterschool Fund:

> J. C. Penney Corporation, Inc., the wholly owned operating subsidiary of J. C. Penney Company, Inc., is one of America's largest department store, catalog, and e-commerce retailers, employing approximately 150,000 associates. As of April 30, 2005, J. C. Penney Corporation, Inc. operated 1,017 JCPenney department stores throughout the United States and Puerto Rico. JCPenney is the nation's largest catalog merchant of general merchandise, and jcpenney.com is one of the largest apparel and home furnishings sites on the Internet.

What struck me about this example was that the about statement had no relevance to the subject of the news release, wristbands. Incidentally you will note in this actual excerpt from a typical J. C. Penney news release that the company's PR people spell the name of the company two different ways: "J. C. Penney" and "JCPenney." I got curious and asked the J. C. Penney/JCPenney corporate communications department to explain why they do this, and I received this explanation via e-mail:

> J. C. Penney Company, Inc. is the legal entity or holding company which [sic] owns J. C. Penney Corporation, Inc. The holding company also owned businesses in Brazil (Lojas Renner Department Stores), the Eckerd drugstore chain, a department store chain in Mexico and Chile, a credit card bank, insurance company and other operations. All of these businesses, with the exception of the domestic department store chain, are no longer owned by J. C. Penney Company, Inc.

> J. C. Penney Corporation, Inc. is the legal entity which owns and runs our domestic JCPenney Department Store chain, jcpenney.com and our catalog business.

Ah, well, heck, I thought. *That makes all the sense in the world. Silly me for asking. That's stuff any journalist needs to know, including the punctuation errors.* Still, what about the relevance of such a convoluted, legalese statement embedded in a news release about wristbands for children? So I telephoned the J. C. Penney/JCPenney corporate communications department.

"It's just something standard we do. All our competitors do, so we must too," I was told. *That's smart. Copy your competitors.* But is it relevant for every news release, I asked? "No, I guess not," was the response, "but we've just gotten into the habit of adding it to all releases."

Sometimes an organization's communications team needs to question bad habits and copycat styles.

Journalists suggest that companies should just focus on "news" in a news release and not use the forum to advertise and promote.

This seems logical, but corporate thinking a compulsive eye always on sales and promotion, takes a different view at many organizations. The position seems to be "if our attorneys think we're going to the edge of believability anyway, we might as well go all the way and use news releases for sales purposes."

In companies where public relations is under the control of the marketing department, the trend of marrying about and safe-harbor statements has gotten completely out of control. Software developer MicroStrategy, for example, includes a voluminous 200-word boilerplate about statement at the end of its news releases, full of puffy adjectives trumpeting the company's glory. The length of their about promotion rivals the length of the actual news content. They are by no means alone.

The about boilerplate is a trend that has become commonplace at too many organizations, which apparently are under the impression that news releases are just another type of sales collateral material.

Among journalists, standard boilerplate potentially creates the impression that a company may not be making the effort to develop anything truly newsworthy except a commercial message embedded in a news release to promote itself.

What organizations don't seem to realize is that news releases are targeted for the news media, not potential customers. News releases are not sales brochures or advertisements or billboards. News releases are intended to announce legitimate *news*.

After all, what's the purpose of the news release — to communicate real news or distribute promotional fluff? If your answer is the latter, consider protecting your organization's credibility by passing the assignment off to the marketing department and advise them to buy an ad.

Veteran C-SPAN television producer Scott Scully wants news releases that are credible and concise. "Send *accurate* information to the assignment desk," he said. "This means the correct date and time ... contact person and *relevant* information."

News releases can be most effective when used to announce timely and relevant information that affects an organization's audiences. In today's highly competitive world, where the image of an organization rests on convincing and accurate words, too much is at stake to mess with credibility by bastardizing a news release for self-promotional agendas.

It all comes back to the traditional intent of a news release, that bridge for communicating with the news media, and understanding, above all, that a release is all about providing accurate news to help journalists develop a story.

If the news release content is accurate, truthful and timely, there is no journalistic or legal reason for a safe-harbor statement. Just tell the news.

And as for the imagined need for that about boilerplate in a news release, let's get real. The unique value and competitive positioning of any company, organization, issue or cause on the planet can be described in fewer than a dozen quotable and memorable words, easily embedded as a phrase within the actual news release copy. If it drones on much longer, it becomes a speech or a full-blown advertorial.

Over and over, journalists say that the best form of media relations is relationship-based, when a person responsible for media relations simply stays in touch with a circle of reporters who are interested in his or her organization. As we have stated earlier in this book, news releases are no substitute for getting to know the right journalists.

News releases are to announce news, not to be used as advertising flyers. Always tell the truth, and you won't need to hide behind an attorney or in a safe harbor that might turn out to be too shallow.

Contentious Words Are Thought Stoppers

I have always loved to read Mark Twain. About the craft of writing, he told a friend, "I notice that you use plain, simple language, short words and brief sentences. That is the way to write English — it is the modern way and the best way. Stick to it; don't let fluff and flowers and verbosity creep in. When you catch an adjective, kill it."

> "I notice that you use plain, simple language, short words and brief sentences. That is the way to write English — it is the modern way and the best way. Stick to it; don't let fluff and flowers and verbosity creep in. When you catch an adjective, kill it." — Mark Twain

It has long been important to many companies and organizations to claim — especially when describing themselves in news releases — that they are "the largest" or "the best" or "the leading" or whatever.

Companies often spend enormous amounts of time guessing the best words to use. They exhaust themselves with such prattling, attempting to make it stick and convince us that they are the greatest outfits on the planet.

Such contentious words seldom fly. Claims to be the best will often cause listeners or readers to stop in their tracks and question whether it's true or not. Organizations need to remember Twain's advice to kill the adjectives.

Remember all the dot-com and technology companies of the late 1990s? With negligible track records or earnings, they all claimed to be "the most advanced" or "the leading integrated service provider." And

where are they now? Their claims were not believable. Ma
not true.

If I were to tell you that I am "the smartest man on eai , your
ability to listen to and believe what I was saying would likely stop at
that point. I might continue talking and provide numerous reasons to
support my claim, but chances are you would still be questioning the
word *smartest*. You wouldn't be listening to me but rather compiling a
list in your mind of the many other people far smarter than me. My
claim would lack credibility, and everything else I might attempt to say
would be dismissed.

It is a natural impulse when we hear boastful words to stop where
we are and immediately question their validity. A company claims to
be outstanding, and we quietly think to ourselves, "Well, I can think of
a dozen other companies that are better," ignoring whatever else the
company tries to say.

When someone or an organization brags in the media, they are not
only being contentious and risking the chance the media might ignore
them as a result; they are also gambling with their credibility. One single contentious word or phrase can stop effective communication. It's
like calling the blind with a 3 and a 5, off suit, in a poker game of
Texas Hold 'Em. You've really got nothing ... but talk.

Attorneys Speak Legalese

With full knowledge that I am entering possibly hostile waters here, I will say that, as a broad and sweeping generalization, attorneys seldom make for good spokespeople when left unchecked. I've seen attorneys make powerful presentations in court only to walk outside the building to stand before a battery of microphones and cameras ... and freeze. Under the media's glare, some attorneys become incapable of putting together a few sentences to summarize their case for a public audience.

I should add quickly that I have worked with some outstanding attorneys who enthusiastically welcomed interview technique coaching, and today do an admirable job whenever in front of a microphone, camera or gaggle of reporters.

The problem for many attorneys who lack a thorough understanding of how to speak with the media, I believe, is the inability to intellectually shift gears from legal speak to a more common language. Perhaps it is a translation challenge. Many attorneys also don't know what a sound bite is, generally don't care and wouldn't know how to compose one if their lives depended on it.

A sound bite is defined as describing your endeavor, precisely and in a captivating way, in one breath — about 16 seconds — using words that are understandable, credible, exciting and memorable.

The news media cherishes sound bites. Reporters agree that a great sound bite will bring a story to life. Today's politicians, it seems, prefer to talk in nothing but sound bites, because they want to make news.

Sound bites are the media relations technique of getting to the bottom line of what you have to say — and unquestionably one of the best ways to get into print and on television and radio newscasts. *Sound bites get to the heart of the story.* Journalists can then always ask more questions and fill in all the details if they choose.

Many attorneys speak primarily *legalese,* a vague-sounding, verbose, ambiguous and somewhat evasive language that not a lot of us, including the news media, understand. The attorneys presumably comprehend what they are saying, and other attorneys may too. Legalese comes from their training. But most of us don't understand legalese; it is not everyday language.

The mixture of legalese with arrogance, too often the signature of attorneys, is a destructive cocktail in media relations. Yet many times we've seen an attorney speaking in what seems like a pompous manner to "set the record straight" on behalf of a client or organization. I don't know about you, but I sometimes find myself wanting to root for the other guy.

There are, of course, exceptions. Reporters enjoy interviewing attorneys who can demonstrate skill at interpreting often-complicated legal opinions and theory into words that are clear and concise. Washington, D.C., attorney Thomas Wilner is one of the best. Wilner has represented Kuwaiti men held at Guantanamo Bay by the United States without access to due process rights, a controversial case with debate that reached the United States Supreme Court.

In discussing that case on the PBS "NewsHour," this is how Wilner responded to a reporter's question about the meaning of habeas corpus:

> Habeas corpus was really a fundamental right developed under the common law. It really was to enforce the rights granted by the Magna Carta. The Magna Carta said that no person shall be deprived of his liberty without jury by his peers and accordance with the law of the land and habeas corpus was developed to enforce that. Really what it does, it requires judicial review, independent review of the facts and circumstances to see whether there's a reason to hold somebody.

In this interview, Wilner translated possibly confusing legal language and terminology clearly into words that everyone can comprehend.

Attorneys like Wilner are important and valuable partners in the news media communication process. They can give essential guidance and suggestions on wording and opinions about legal issues. They can help to identify potential minefields and problems well in advance. But the language of law needs to be translated into words, phrases and thoughts that more effectively communicate with the key audiences we are seeking to reach, inform and motivate, including the media.

In my work, both as a journalist and in public relations, I've found only a handful of attorneys who are skilled at delivering concise messages to the media in layman's terms. Rather than working with communicators to find interesting ways to generate coverage, so many attorneys actually impede the image and media relations efforts of their clients or companies by coming up with laundry lists of usually improbable scenarios and finding reasons why doing anything would be a bad idea.

Lawyers are too prone to thinking defensively and trying to persuade an organization into "no comment" mode, even when there's nothing to fear in communicating with the news media. No comment only builds fear and mistrust about an organization. In media relations, it's not an option.

Lawyers have a place in the media relations process, and we are starting to see change on the horizon as more attorneys recognize the power and value of knowing how their words can make news.

Those working in media relations should establish working relationships with attorneys. Seek their counsel, consider the opportunities, and think about what's best for your organization and your audiences and your stakeholders. And if you are stuck with an attorney as a spokesperson, get them some media training *first*.

When dealing with the news media, we need to communicate as clearly and accurately as possible. Legal speak is seldom convincing in working with the media, and all too often can cause confusion by getting tangled up in its own complex language and jargon.

Media Relations Field Guide

The Pillars of Media Relations

Think of the pillars of effective news media relations as three legs on a stool that allow you to stand above the crowd and be seen. Take away one or two legs, and you'll fall off. Add too many legs, and the stool becomes awkward and unmanageable. Here are the three pillars:

Pillar 1: The Media Relations Plan. A plan gives focus to your purpose and your objectives. Why would any organization ever consider launching an outreach program, issuing a news release or making any public statement without some sort of plan that provides purpose, relevance and context?

Without a plan, public statements or promotional announcements usually lack focus and could actually work against fulfillment of an organization's overall marketing and business objectives. You could be compromising your company's reputation. So why would you say anything in public without a plan? I cannot think of any reason except for carelessness or ambivalence about your organization's image. Nonetheless many companies crank out news release after news release, often without rhyme or reason.

Effective media relations begins with a carefully thought-out plan to competitively position an organization. The plan embraces the overall corporate vision and objectives and gives focus, purpose and reason to a communications effort. It does not begin with tactics or with copying tactics that you've seen other people use to boost visibility in the media. It begins with asking yourself candid and tough questions that will help you really put your fingers on the distinct pulse of your organization and identify precisely the right ways and the best words to enhance your image before key audiences. Some of those questions are:

- What's so special about your organization that makes it stand out from anyone else, and who cares beyond the company parking lot?

- What are the things about your company that appeal most to the people who really matter outside and who rely on your organization, such as customers and stakeholders?

- How do you want your company talked about, in clear, jargon-free words? In other words, how do you think your best customer might describe why you were chosen over a competitor?

- What is genuinely newsworthy about your organization and what it does or produces?

Think of a media relations plan as a beacon that will guide important audiences to your organization. A media relations plan mirrors the objectives of a company's business plan and works to bring the strategic business plan to life more efficiently and more compellingly than any other method.

The plan's components are straightforward:

- *Situation overview.* A few paragraphs to summarize the lay of the land, competitive environment, challenges and obstacles, advantages and opportunities. This is your opportunity to say, "Here's what we're going to do and how we're going to make it happen."

- *Audiences.* A list of all audiences that you intend to reach through your media relations initiative — internal and external, public and highly specialized. I've always observed a natural tendency to create a list that's too long yet often omits the news media. Sometimes we will list an audience group that's no longer relevant to our business. Here's your chance to fine-tune that list and reduce it to the essentials.

- *Positioning message.* The introductory sentence or two that distinctly and clearly differentiates you from your competitors and will work to capture the attention of your key audiences. (For more on positioning messages, see the next chapter.)

- *Objectives.* Preferably three and certainly no more than four goals that reflect and complement the aim of your organization's business plan. Begin each objective with an active word, such as *boost* or *enhance* or *create*. There's an old style of beginning each objective with the word *to*.

- *Strategies.* There must be a specific strategy for achieving each objective. This is where you describe in detail how you intend to achieve the objectives — in other words, how you plan to get from here to there. Remember that you cannot list an objective without a strategy for making it happen.

- *Tactics.* The unique and distinctive action points that will bring your strategies to life in order to achieve the objectives.

- *Measurement.* The plan must have a mechanism to demonstrate tangible results. Elements can include an upward trend in news stories, increased Web site traffic and more unsolicited contact from journalists. Create a *measurement matrix*, a chart that tracks each component and clearly shows achievements.

Be mindful of not allowing tactics to drive the planning process. *Tactics are the fun side of planning, while objectives and strategies require more thought.* Consequently people all too often jump to tactics that may or may not be relevant to the plan. That could lead to wasted time, wrong strategic directions and costly mistakes.

Let me digress for a moment to talk about objectives, strategies and tactics and provide an example.

An objective might be driving to the beach for the weekend.

A strategy is how you are going to make it happen, such as planning the shortest trip at the best time to avoid traffic. There is always just one strategy to achieve each objective.

Tactics are the actions, items or steps needed to bring a strategy to life and for accomplishing an end, such as, in this case, finding the car keys, putting your suitcase in the trunk and finding a roadmap.

During the process of developing a plan, the right tactics will naturally reveal themselves. Chances are you can even identify clever new tactics that will become distinctive to your organization. So even if someone else currently has an advantage over you in the area of media relations, it's realistic to expect to gain the upper hand, because many people don't bother with developing a smart media relations plan. I've found that most people think only about tactics, such as a news release, and hope that will solve everything. Before you think about tactics, think big. Have a strategy.

Once you've launched that process, you will begin to see your company through a new set of eyes, with 20/20 vision, focused on the essence of what's important. You will no longer find it relevant to think of your organization in terms of competitors but rather as a unique organization of talented people who are part of something big.

Pillar 2: Be Original. While it always helps to know your competition, ignore what they are saying and how they are saying it. Although a competitor may do something cool, it may not be either smart or effective. If there's a news story about them, and you are not mentioned, forget it. As with the city bus, another opportunity will soon come along before you know it. If you copy or react to the featured organization, you have, by default, put yourself in second place, made yourself a "wannabe" in the media's eyes. The news media and the public don't like wannabes.

Ignore how the competition talks to the media. Chart new territory. Be original and imaginative, because you are smarter and savvier than they are.

There's too much competitive clutter out there in the marketplace these days. You cannot afford to be ordinary. Throw out conventional wisdom and traditional approaches to media relations. I've often said that conventional wisdom is a code phrase for dull and predictable.

Challenge the claims and promises of your public relations agency, if you have one. Forget news releases and expensive media kits. Don't fall into the trap of feeling compelled to announce every little event that happens at your place. Your organization has special things to say, so why say them in a predictable and boring fashion?

An essential part of being original is using clever visuals. If you want to quickly leapfrog your brand out ahead of your competition, think about three things: visuals … visuals … visuals. Nothing captures the media's attention faster than great pictures. When it comes to what makes it on the air, a TV news producer most often will go with a second-class story that has great visuals over a better story without visuals. That's just the way journalism works, and it's not going to change. Television news is driven completely by visuals over content.

These days print journalism is more focused on appealing visuals as well. *USA Today* created a whole new way of using color, graphics and pictures when it debuted in the early 1980s, and most other newspapers and magazines have followed suit and improved on the trend. The fastest way into the business section of a major daily newspaper is with a story that has a compelling photo. Most business editors could not care less about the introduction of a new automobile, but when the car maker's chief executive officer and his top designer are seated on the front of the car in a photo, and a crisply written story about the smart teaming of the two executives is provided with it, editors pay attention.

Pillar 3: Tell the Truth. Regardless of the situation and circumstances, using accuracy and candor in dealing with the media is always the best route.

Ever since the technology bubble burst in the early part of this decade, pundits have debated the possible reasons why it happened. Certainly there were numerous financial and market forces at work, not the least of which was the massive overvaluation of many technology stock offerings, based on nothing more than a promise and a prayer. But the most fundamental reason, in my opinion, was the lack of truth in how so many tech companies were promoted to the news media.

In the rock 'n' roll environment of high-flying late 1990s, when everything about technology companies — literally everything from balance sheets and business plans to marketing claims and stock performance — was overstated or nonexistent, communications with the media was also hyped. The climate was right. Business reporters, bored of covering the traditional stories, were all of a sudden being hustled by exciting new companies and ideas. They took the bait and bought all the hype. The stories seemed too good not to believe. Everyone from venture capitalists to analysts to the markets was seemingly validating the high-flying news. Of course, as it turned out, the venture capitalists and analysts and markets were all making tons of money directly from the tech companies.

But in the end, contempt for the truth spelled downfall. Ultimately the truth will come out. From the perspective of journalists I have spoken with, failed technology companies have no one to blame but themselves for their demise. Greed eclipsed truth and accuracy. And we have seen the fallout: markets and investors skittish of any tech venture, even at the expense of the handful of companies out there who might be making money with a unique product or service. The once ever-so-smug leaders of tech during that era nearly killed an entire industry by not telling the truth.

In the world of effective media relations, imaginative ideas and the truth win out over conventional wisdom and hype every day of the week.

Mission Statements Versus Positioning Messages

A heating and air-conditioning contractor handed me his card as we discussed the price of updating the system in my home. There on the bottom of his card was his company's mission statement. It said the company had "vision," was "dedicated to serving customers" and a few other nice things, in about 18 words.

But the card didn't say what I really wanted to know: why I should choose this company over any other heating and air-conditioning outfit. That would be a *positioning message*.

If you really read them closely, mission statements don't make a lot of sense.

They are frequently a pastiche of buzzwords designed to sound lofty, reassuring, authoritative and … well, boring. The end result too often is a "Who cares?" effect.

This heating and air-conditioning company and many others proudly trumpet mission statements rather than focusing on the distinctiveness of the products or services they offer. They are bragging from their perspective rather than understanding my needs as a customer.

Most professional image and reputation management advisors counsel clients to spend minimal time on mission statements and instead to focus real thought on positioning messages, where the words can create genuine competitive differentiation.

Why, you ask, is this important to know in media relations? Because one of our primary goals in approaching the news media is to communicate a subtle differentiating message about our organization to audiences reached by the media. We not only want to be reported on but also remembered.

What's the difference between a mission statement and a positioning message? There's a big difference. Here's a guide:

A mission statement tells people who are close to your organization where you want to go in a perfect world. It is visionary, idealistic and filled with words that tell people you are nice. It describes the future — a quest for growth or a promise of unparalleled integrity. Who can argue with that?

> A mission statement tells people who are close to your organization where you want to go in a perfect world. It is visionary, idealistic and filled with words that tell people you are nice.

Let's take a look at a couple of examples of mission statements, these from not-for-profit conservation organizations. The mission statement for the National Wildlife Federation is "to protect wildlife for our children's future."

By comparison, the mission statement of the World Wildlife Fund, National Wildlife Federation's competitor, is "The conservation of nature. Using the best available scientific knowledge and advancing that knowledge where we can, we work to preserve the diversity and abundance of life on Earth and the health of ecological systems."

While both mission statements are lofty and idealistic, they are general to the point of being dull. They lack the ability to competitively differentiate either group. Neither mission statement manages to tell an audience, "Yes, this phrase is specifically about National Wildlife Federation versus World Wildlife Fund." In fact you could swap these statements between organizations and few of us would know the difference.

While I chose these mission statements at random, they are typical of most you will find. Mission statements don't, by definition, talk about where you are today or your competitive edge, but only what you hope to achieve.

Mission statements, like too many advertising, promotional and media relations claims, could apply just as easily to an organization's competitors.

You see, despite a common misperception, mission statements are intended to target and possibly inspire mostly internal audiences — employees, stakeholders, boards of directors and business partners. While the purpose of mission statements may be high-minded, they are by nature never very exciting, because they are future-focused. They do not create competitive positioning for an organization's image today. A mission statement is not a part of marketing communications or media relations — primarily because it does not address what's special about your organization versus that of a competitor.

On the other hand, a positioning message focuses on today and, if crafted carefully, will incisively leave an audience with a clear understanding of who you are. It describes what is distinctive about your organization that will give it a competitive advantage today. It states how you wish to be perceived today.

> A positioning message focuses on today and, if crafted carefully, will incisively leave an audience with a clear understanding of who you are. It describes what is distinctive about your organization that will give it a competitive advantage today. It states how you wish to be perceived today.

Most important, a positioning message is a competitive differentiator that helps a customer choose you over someone else. It's a simple message, not a slogan or tagline, that gets to the core of what's special about your organization. It is a pillar of media relations.

Here's a story about one organization's costly misuse of a mission statement.

When I began working with leaders of 4-H on a major and ongoing initiative to reshape the image and brand of that national youth development organization, I walked into an environment that had only known mission statements and slogans. Like many other such groups, 4-H had changed its mission statement so often and had come up with slogans so frequently that the general, nondescript words had lost all meaning.

Incidentally the 4-H organization had spent hundreds of thousands of dollars on research and consultants and branding experts, and all they ever ended up with were slogans. One 4-H branding campaign, developed by the Advertising Council, promoted the slogan "Are You Into It?" The effort cost the youth group a fortune in advertising, and back-end testing revealed it had actually damaged the reputation of the 4-H brand.

Surveys conducted before and after the campaign revealed a 10 percent drop in respect for the organization's image as a result of the branding effort. It was found that the "Are You Into It?" phrase was so bland and nondescriptive that it painted 4-H as a boring organization with no special qualities or appeal. In other words, "Are You Into It?" communicated little value and was so general-sounding that it meant nothing. It demoted the 4-H reputation.

Yet 4-H's struggle to find its distinctive brand identification went much deeper. There are over 1,000 4-H related Web sites on the Internet, and, as a result, there are seemingly just about as many descriptions of 4-H. Many people know the brand and 4-H clover logo, but few have an understanding of what 4-H does as an organization. The 4-H organization had become its own competition.

Leaders had invested hours revising their mission statement, and yet they continued to fail at attracting new members and funding. In fact both were on a decline. This decline can be attributed partly to the use of a mission statement in attempts to market 4-H to new audiences. By its very nature the statement lacked differentiating characteristics that might give anyone exciting reasons to choose 4-H over another youth organization.

The 4-H organization lacked a positioning message that would that would provide the chance to break through competitive clutter and influentially recalibrate the 4-H brand.

I believed the answer could be found by talking with the youth of 4-H around America. The 4-H organization had previously spent a fortune on market research and advertising yet had never interviewed their No. 1 and most important audience — the youth who belong to 4-H — to determine how they might describe the 4-H experience. Everything to that point had been from the perspective of adults, not youth. Grownups trying to figure out how to capture the attention of kids seldom works, as any parent knows.

My strategy was to find a way to describe the unique soul of 4-H in words that were clear and adjective-free and left no one out. In all of 4-H's branding efforts in the past, no one had ever gone out and interviewed the young people of the organization in such a detailed manner.

As I traveled from state to state chatting with groups of 4-H youth and listening to how they described the 4-H adventure, I heard the same words being used by many youths, whether they were in Madison, Georgia, or Davis, California. I call these words an organization's *common-thread words*.

The 4-H youth were using common-thread words like "community" and "young people." They said they were "learning" by working together in a mentoring environment with adults. What were they learning? I asked. "Leadership, citizenship and life skills," they answered.

During my interviews I found it interesting that 4-H members often referred to their peers as "young people" as we discussed ways to describe 4-H to an outside audience. The adult leaders of the 4-H organization, by contrast, usually referred to the young people as "kids."

I listened to the youth of 4-H, and they told me that "4-H is a community of young people across America who are learning leadership, citizenship and life skills."

The youth had defined one of the strongest positioning messages I had ever heard, and they had used distinctive words from *their* perspective, not from the viewpoint of adults talking about "kids."

The new positioning message said it all about America's oldest youth-development organization, and it said it in clear and simple language. It was an appealing message upon which to build a media relations campaign. Most of all, the message centered, for the first time ever, on the *value* of 4-H to young people. Previous attempts at messages had centered around the organization, which at the end of the day, no one really cared about.

Before long the entire organization was using the positioning message. It spread like wildfire. A young 4-H girl stood at a podium before the governor of Indiana and 300 people to dedicate remodeled 4-H buildings at the Indiana State Fair, and she began by saying, "4-H is a community of young people across America who are learning leadership, citizenship and life skills."

The 4-H youth put it on T-shirts. County agents use it on their e-mail signature lines. It is being used everywhere and at most levels of the organization. And the result is that wider audiences are becoming aware of the scope and impact of 4-H today in helping America's young people.

The positioning message sets you apart from your competitors. And here's a tip: To sharpen your appeal, narrow your position. We cannot be all things to all people. To be successful, we must focus on one thing and be the best at it.

> To sharpen your appeal, narrow your position. We cannot be all things to all people. To be successful, we must focus on one thing and be the best at it.

One thing, you say? Yes. Your organization might do many other things, but be recognized for excelling at one thing. Get people talking about that, and you will win competitively.

Remember all those "and more" businesses that couldn't figure out what they were? "Windows, Doors and More." "Yarns, Sewing and More." "Electronics, Hobbies and More."

Many of those places are gone simply because they failed to build a reputation of being outstanding in one area. They tried to be all things to all people.

Wal-Mart, you might argue, is one of those "and more" businesses. Not so. Even though they may sell just about everything imaginable, the company has for decades narrowly focused on one competitive message: "Always the Lowest Price. Always." That's Wal-Mart's positioning message, and they own it. In an ever-changing marketplace, they've been consistent, and they've won. Their promise has been fulfilled across America, and it has given them the edge.

Electronic Tip Sheets

During the United States presidential campaign of 2004, Senator John Kerry, the Democratic candidate, played up his distinguished military service in Vietnam, including receiving a Purple Heart for being wounded. The strategy underscored patriotic commitment to his country while reminding voters that his opponent, George W. Bush, had managed to avoid going to Vietnam.

Kerry made it a centerpiece of his campaign. In speech after speech, week after week, Kerry talked about his military service, even though it had been over 30 years ago. He said that because of what he experienced in Vietnam, he had come to the conclusion that the war was wrong. When he got home from the war, he joined a group called the Vietnam Veterans Against the War, to protest America's involvement in the Southeast Asian conflict.

As the presidential campaign of 2004 heated up, about 200 Vietnam-era veterans, all of them conservatives, formed the group Swift Boat Veterans for Truth or SBVT and held news conferences, ran ads, launched a blog and endorsed a book titled *Unfit for Command* that questioned Kerry's service record and his military awards. Several SBVT members were in the same unit with Kerry, but only one, Stephen Gardner, served on the same boat. Other SBVT members included two of Kerry's former commanding officers, Grant Hibbard and George Elliott. Hibbard and Elliott alleged, respectively, that Kerry's first Purple Heart and Silver Star were undeserved. In addition members of SBVT questioned his other medals, his truthfulness in testimony about the war and his involvement with Vietnam Veterans Against the War.

The more Kerry spoke of his war record, the more traction his opponents got. The SBVT's most influential tactic was its online blog. Within minutes of each Kerry speech, the Swift Boat Veterans for Truth managed to reach the news media with timely sound bites and rebuttals to his specific remarks via their online weapon. The effect was not only to diminish what he had said but also to extend the accusations about his patriotism and truthfulness. Their blog worked to undermine Kerry's credibility during the campaign. Soon the candidate's distinguished military service was seen as a liability.

Defenders of Kerry's war record, including nearly all of his surviving former crewmates, countered that organizers of SBVT had close ties to the Bush presidential campaign, and that the accusations were false and politically motivated. But their voices of support came too late and were delivered via the slower, old-fashioned method of news conferences. Contemporary media relations defeated 1980s-style efforts at every turn. The blog's increasingly shrill criticism of Kerry worked to overshadow the fact that Kerry's opponent, George W. Bush, had completely dodged being sent to the Vietnam War. Kerry's defenders didn't stand a chance.

Blogs have quickly become influential as a tool to inform, influence, manage and, in a few cases, manipulate the news media. For public relations professionals and people assigned the task of communicating with the news media, nothing is better than having established contacts and relationships with journalists. Blogs help to streamline communication with reporters and increase our voice through the news media. The overriding reality is that blogs, while certainly not the ultimate solution, have become an accepted and influential communications method for practicing media relations.

Blogs started out somewhat humbly on the Internet just a couple of years ago, largely as a novelty for individual self-expression. They have become the fastest-developing segment of the Internet as people find it far easier to establish a voice online with a blog than with a more cumbersome, expensive and time-consuming Web site.

A traditional Web site, typically comprising multiple pages and complex organizational structure, requires special developmental software on your computer and some level of expertise about coding. Sites are put together like a complicated family tree, starting with a home page and often going in many directions. Over time it can become a very large tapestry of pages. Changing Web site content takes time and can be complicated to do. It's not uncommon to hear of a Web site that has grown to thousands of pages.

Blogs, on the other hand, are much simpler. The software resides on a remote Internet server, and you never need to really bother with the software or learning programming code, but only focus on writing the content. It's easy to sign on and update a blog in a couple of minutes, and it can be done with any computer with online capability around the world. You can begin to see why it's such an effective tool in media relations.

The news media has stampeded toward the use of blogs, both to get the news to their audiences and to monitor as *electronic tip sheets* for possible stories.

When Hurricane Katrina struck the Gulf Coast of the United States in the summer of 2005, news updates were coming so fast that news organizations, such as MSNBC, replaced their Web sites with blogs in order to get developments online faster. Updating a Web site, they found, takes too much time.

The online participatory encyclopedia, Wikipedia, is recognized for providing the most current definitions of new media, new trends and new technology. There, the definition of a "blog" is:

> A web-based publication consisting primarily of periodic articles (normally, but not always, in reverse chronological order). Although most early blogs were manually updated, tools to automate the maintenance of such sites made them accessible to a much larger population, and the use of some sort of browser-based software is now a typical aspect of "blogging."

Blogs range in scope from individual diaries to arms of political campaigns, media programs, and corporations. They range in scale from the writings of one occasional author (known as a blogger), to the collaboration of a large community of writers. Many weblogs enable visitors to leave public comments, which can lead to a community of readers centered around the blog; others are non-interactive. The totality of weblogs or blog-related Web sites is often called the blogosphere. When a large amount of activity, information and opinion erupts around a particular subject or controversy in the blogosphere, it is sometimes called a blogstorm or blog swarm.

The trend is clear for those of us who work with journalists to develop news stories: blogs have become accepted by the news media as *electronic tip sheets* that can provide timely, relevant and essential background material. The reason they are popular is the format. Unlike a traditional Web site with a spider web of dozens, if not thousands, of pages that a visitor has to navigate through, a blog is simple and organized.

Think of a blog as one page of your journal with one or more entries. It's a good method of presenting a timely issue or point of view. You can make each entry as short or as long as you wish. Through the intuitive options of blog services — such as Six Apart's TypePad or Google's Blogger — you can upload photographs, arrange your entries in descending or ascending order, and efficiently archive blog postings by week or month. For visitors the presentation is clear, intuitive and right there before their eyes. No more wading through a Web site to find what they need.

NBC News correspondent George Lewis told me, "I think that those of us in the MSM (mainstream media) are paying a whole lot of attention these days to blogs and podcasts because they often function as an early-warning radar about major stories. For instance, when I was researching a story recently on avian influenza, I routinely checked several blogs devoted to the subject. That gave me some names of researchers working in the field and enabled me to contact them directly.

"I tend to think of the blogs as an electronic tip sheet with stuff that always needs to be verified by traditional journalistic methods."

> "I tend to think of the blogs as an electronic tip sheet with stuff that always needs to be verified by traditional journalistic methods." — George Lewis, correspondent, NBC News

Blogs can be more powerful than tip sheets. A tremendous political controversy was sparked by a blog that reported inappropriate racial remarks by Senate Majority Leader Trent Lott at the 100th birthday party for Senator Strom Thurmond. The event was covered but not reported by mainstream media — at least, the mainstream media did not report it until the story was picked up by *Instapundit.com*, a blog written by University of Tennessee law professor Glenn Reynolds, and by *Talking Points Memo*, a blog run by political reporter Joshua Micah Marshall.

The New York Times columnist Paul Krugman wrote that Marshall's blog was "more than anyone else, responsible for making Trent Lott's offensive remarks the issue they deserve to be." As a result of the ensuing controversy, Lott resigned from his powerful post in Congress.

San Francisco-based technology reporter Dan Gillmor has written that "in a world of blogs, podcasts, video mash-ups, interactive maps, and so much more, the nature of corporate communications must change from top-down control to multi-directional openness — from lecture to conversation. If all that is daunting, however, keep in mind that the new options are available to the newsmakers and the PR people advising them, not just the bloggers.

"Blogs are all the rage, and I encourage their use as part of the external — and internal — communications process. Unlike press releases, which tend to read as if they'd been composed by the mating of a computer and lawyer, good blogs have a distinctly human voice. They are conversational almost by definition."

> "Unlike press releases, which tend to read as if they'd been composed by the mating of a computer and lawyer, good blogs have a distinctly human voice. They are conversational almost by definition." — Dan Gillmor, journalist and blogster

Gillmor has come up with a brilliant definition of blogs. He calls them "grassroots journalism … for the people, by the people."

In London, Jon Williams is a visionary television news manager who is in charge of charting the future of the news business at the BBC — a future not 10 years from now, but potentially next week.

"Online blogs give critics a platform," he wrote me in an e-mail. "No longer do they need a newspaper to publish a 'letter to the editor.' Individuals can publish [on their own blog] and be damned. We're witness to the democratization of newsgathering."

When I read his words, I thought, *Wow, what an exciting time for practicing media relations.* Not only do blogs give "critics a platform," we in media relations can take the spotlight and make news as well.

In many ways we're seeing the beginnings of a more level playing field between journalists and those of us who make our livings pitching stories on behalf of employers and clients to the media. The lines of communications are opening, perhaps more than ever, because of technology.

No one knows this more than French journalist Julien Pain, who, since the late 1990s, has been looking for more influential ways of using the Internet to help give voice to ordinary people, especially persecuted people, around the world. Few people know more about blogs than Pain, who heads the Internet Freedom desk at Paris-based Reporters Without Borders, an organization devoted to championing freedom of the press around the world. The group has six offices globally and maintains a trilingual — French, English and Spanish — Web site that functions like a press-freedom news agency.

Pain told me that blogs are not the type of revolution that the Internet created but rather a better and easier way for people to communicate online. Other technological forms will come along, he said, but for now, blogs are the best tool for people whose press freedoms have been squelched or controlled.

> "A blog gives everyone, regardless of education or technical skill, the chance to publish material. This means boring or disgusting blogs will spring up as fast as good and interesting ones." — Julien Pain, Internet Freedom, Reporters Without Borders

Under Pain's leadership, Reporters Without Borders has undertaken an ambitious project to encourage more ordinary people to begin speaking out through blogs. To support the project, he has published a comprehensive document on the power and influence of blogs, the *Handbook for Bloggers and Cyber-Dissidents*. Supported through Reporters Without Borders' Web site — rsf.org — the document offers "practical advice and technical tips to help bloggers stay anonymous and get around censorship."

This well-written handbook not only is an important document and worth reading for cyber-dissidents in such places as Iran, China, Nepal and Tunisia, but is also enlightening information for anyone in the field of media relations who wants to learn more about the influence of blogs. Here are some of Julien Pain's words:

> Blogs get people excited. Or else they disturb and worry them. Some people distrust them. Others see them as the vanguard of a new information revolution. One thing's for sure: they're rocking the foundations of the media in countries as different as the United States, China and Iran.

> It's too soon to really know what to think of blogs. We've been reading newspapers, watching TV and listening to the radio for decades now and we've learned how to immediately tell what's news and what's comment, to distinguish a tabloid "human inter-

est" magazine from a serious one and an entertainment programme from a documentary.

We don't have such antennae to figure out blogs. These "online diaries" are even more varied than the mainstream media and it's hard to know which of them is a news site, which a personal forum or one that does serious investigation or one that's presenting junk evidence. It's difficult to separate the wheat from the chaff.

Some bloggers will gradually develop their own ethical standards to become more credible and win public confidence. But the Internet is still full of unreliable information and people exchanging insults. A blog gives everyone, regardless of education or technical skill, the chance to publish material. This means boring or disgusting blogs will spring up as fast as good and interesting ones.

But blogging is a powerful tool of freedom of expression that has enthused millions of ordinary people. Passive consumers of information have become energetic participants in a new kind of journalism.

Bloggers are often the only real journalists in countries where the mainstream media is censored or under pressure. Only they provide independent news, at the risk of displeasing the government and sometimes courting arrest. Plenty of bloggers have been hounded or thrown in prison.

A key section of the handbook focuses on the subject of ethics: "What Ethics Should Bloggers Have?" That part was written by California-based journalist and blog pioneer Dan Gillmor:

> Not all bloggers do journalism. Most do not. But when they do, they should be ethical.
>
> Does this mean they must subscribe to some kind of ethical code? Not necessarily.
>
> The professional journalism world is awash in ethics codes. Some are longer than the United States Constitution, trying to anticipate every possible breach. Others are short and succinct, offering more

positive guidance. The cyber-journalist Web site has adapted for bloggers an ethics code from the Society of Professional Journalists, an American group. It is a solid and worthy effort.

All ethics codes are created for one essential purpose: to instill trust. If a reader (or viewer or listener) cannot trust the report, there is usually little reason to bother in the first place. The exception, of course, is looking at material that is known to be unethical, as much for instructional purposes — we can learn a great deal from watching unethical people's behavior — as to gain true knowledge.

For me, ethics is about something quite simple: honor. Within that word, however, is a great deal of territory. But unless we act with honor we cannot expect people's trust.

In American journalism, trust is often associated with a standard we call "objectivity" — the idea that an article should offer balance and nuance, giving the reader the chance to make up his or her own mind. I believe objectivity is a worthy but unattainable goal, because we all bring our own biases to everything we do.

In a world of new journalism, where we shift from a lecture to much more of a conversation, ethical journalism depends less on codes of ethics than the values and principles that are a foundation for honorable journalism.

There are pillars of good journalism: thoroughness, accuracy, fairness, transparency and independence.

> "Ethics is about something quite simple: honor. Within that word, however, is a great deal of territory. But unless we act with honor we cannot expect people's trust." — Dan Gillmor, journalist and blogger

As I was reading Gillmor's words, I was reminded that a few blogs in recent years have made headlines by smearing reputations and manipulating news media coverage, like the so-called Swift Boat Veterans for Truth. They had online agendas, often political, with the purpose of corrupting facts and undermining trust. That aside, online blogs as effective and important tools for media relations have an exciting future.

For public relations professionals and people assigned the task of communicating with the news media, blogs are a persuasive and innovative device. They help to simplify communication with reporters, level the playing field in working with journalists and strengthen our voice through the media.

Media relations today, because of such emerging technology, gives individuals, businesses and public relations people more of an opportunity to be transparent. This leads to more openness, better communications and increased credibility. We now have the opportunity to be in control and manage a story rather than surrender control and play catch-up.

Through a growing number of online services, you can start a blog in just a matter of minutes, and the cost is either nominal or free from a variety of providers. The California-based company Six Apart, for example, is a blog pioneer with their popular service called TypePad, where you can quickly set up corporate and personal blogs. TypePad is used by everyone from news organizations to politicians to real estate agents. In less time than it might have taken people a century ago to wait their turn to stand on a soapbox in town square, you can have your own blog on the Internet.

"The news machines are hungry beasts that need filling," Jon Williams of BBC News in London has told me. "Changing technologies allow the broadcasters to go live, from more places, more often than ever before." Blogs have become an accepted method of delivering information directly to a reporter's computer.

Another new tool for media relations is a *podcast*. But first a story on how one person has made international news with this simple and inexpensive online communications device.

Father Roderick Vonhögen, a Catholic priest of the Archdiocese of Utrecht, The Netherlands, has jumped quickly from obscurity to popularity in the media spotlight as one of the most interesting podcasters on the Internet. At a time when the Catholic Church struggles for members and to regain its reputation, Father Vonhögen managed to make the connection between trendy online technology, iPods and God. He calls it "Godcasting," and his related blog, *CatholicInsider.com*, reflects that he is building an audience.

What is a podcast, you ask? Let me explain. The editors of the *New Oxford American Dictionary* define *podcast* as

> A digital recording of a radio broadcast or similar program, made available on the Internet for downloading to a personal audio player.

Incidentally the editors found the word *podcast* to be so popular that they named it "word of the year" in 2005.

Wikipedia, the free online encyclopedia, defines *podcast* this way:

> Podcasting is the distribution of audio or video files, such as radio programs or music videos, over the Internet using either RSS or Atom syndication for listening on mobile devices and personal computers. The term podcast, like "radio," can mean both the content and the method of delivery.

"RSS" and "Atom" are Web feed formats for providing content on blogs.

Steve Jobs, the authentic visionary who runs the computer company Apple, once called podcasting "TiVo for radio." That was a good description, except that Apple subsequently introduced an iPod that also plays video. Just as TiVo's groundbreaking digital video recorder has given people control over their TV viewing, podcasting lets you pick what kinds of audio and video programs you want to watch and listen to — and when. Because podcasts are distributed over the Internet, anyone can create a podcast, like a blog.

To call podcasting popular is an understatement. With the soaring use of small Apple iPods by people of all ages and walks of life around the world, podcasts are the ultimate method of customizing news and information content, depending on personal interests. Everyone, including major corporations and news organizations, is scrambling to find their podcasting niche and capture a piece of the audience.

Podcasts and the spin-offs of podcasts are another example of the trend toward participatory journalism. Citizen journalists are creating programs on every imaginable issue or interest. Podcasts that contain timely and exclusive material can themselves become the subject of coverage by the mainstream news media. Podcasts are already making news.

If you have something on your mind and want to share it with other people who you believe might be interested, you can become a podcaster, right alongside such journalists as Maureen Dowd at *The New York Times* or Michael A. Hiltzik at the *Los Angeles Times* or hundreds of news organizations and journalists and thousands of individuals around the world.

All you need is an inexpensive digital recorder or a microphone that will connect to the USB slot on your computer. Download software, often free, that will allow you to record, edit and produce finished programs on your computer, and you are in business. Podcasts can be uploaded to any number of a growing ring of Internet sites that accept, list and make them available for download.

Many podcasters, like Father Vonhögen, distribute their audio stories, news and features via their own blogs. As the Dutch priest travels Europe, his reports most often focus on timely subjects, like the election of a new pope when he was visiting Rome.

"I just finished editing and uploading the first podcast in the history of podcasting," Father Vonhögen posted on his blog, "that will let you witness the presentation of a new pope. Hear the excitement of the crowd, the music, the applause, and the first words of Pope Benedict XVI 'live' from Saint Peter's Square!"

Clearly the good father may be a servant of God but has a flair for worldly publicity. Father Vonhögen, as well as other successful podcasters, know that the secret is to promote podcasts using a related blog or simple Web site so that the reports can be showcased and easily downloaded.

Other reports and "soundseeing" tours by Father Vonhögen are downright hip and savvy, like his accounts of the Blognomics Congress in Amsterdam and meeting with alternative musicians, like singer Anne Davis.

His reports are well-produced and actually sound much like the features you might hear on National Public Radio. He makes the most of natural sound, short clips of interviews and music. The reports are spontaneous and real, and they capture a special moment of an event. He takes you with him on his travels through the podcasts. Father Roderick is unquestionably a citizen reporter in today's media world. In interviews with the media, he's already promoting video podcasts, just as soon as he finds funding for the needed technical gear.

If a Catholic priest can figure out how to stand in the spotlight of the world media stage, create an ever-growing library of feature stories and both promote and control his message, so can you.

Here's how the concept of a podcast can be used in media relations: Let's say the CEO of your company wants to make a statement to the news media, and your job is to get him on radio newscasts. Rather than hold a news conference, which may not be covered by radio stations these days because they may no longer have enough field reporters to send, you can do all the legwork for the radio newsroom yourself and provide a story that contains precisely the message you want to hear on radio.

Establishing a trusted relationship with radio news operations by getting to know them is the first step. That way they can put a face to a name when you call up and say you have a news story.

Simply interview your CEO or spokesperson about your organization's story on your own, making sure you get a concise sound bite that covers all the important points. It's easily accomplished by using an inexpensive digital recorder.

Copy the recorded statement to your computer, using an audio recording and editing program, such as Audacity. Audacity is a free download from the Internet and extremely easy to use. Edit out any mistakes or pauses and upload the finished recording in a broadcast quality format, such as MP3, to the news section of your Web site. Then it's just a matter of notifying radio newsrooms that they can download the statement from the Web site. Another alternative is simply e-mailing it to them. It is astonishingly easy.

When you get skilled at this technique and provide the radio news media with crisp sound bites, about 15 seconds in length, rather than a long-winded minute or two, you will find the shorter version will be used most often. This is important: Give the news media what they normally will use. If a radio newscast typically runs 15-second clips, give them a 15-second clip. What you are doing is more effectively managing the image — the brand — of your company. You are controlling the message — the actual words — in a timely and relevant way.

Unfortunately it's a common and sometimes costly mistake in media relations to give the media too many irrelevant details. Focus only on the story you are pitching, not a menu of stories. Remember, we are in an era when it's our job to help the media to develop a story. So give them the story that they need, avoiding PR fluff. When you dump too much material on the media, you are giving a reporter or editor choices, and try as they might, they could get the story wrong simply because you didn't focus on the message.

Consider all the uses in media relations, particularly with radio news stations, for *brief* audio sound bites that easily can be included in newscasts and build publicity for your organization, cause or agenda. News/talk radio stations, many of them with newscasts around the clock, are constantly hungry for content and material. When you establish credibility with these broadcast newsrooms, the sky is the limit, because you have essentially become one of their field reporters, providing news.

You have become a citizen journalist and the spectrum of possible stories is limited only by your imagination. Here are some examples:

- A politician can issue a reasoned response to remarks of an opponent within moments and possibly defuse adverse coverage.

- A corporation facing the recall of a consumer product can provide timely and accurate details and demonstrate genuine concern.

- A school system can reach parents through the radio news media with a controlled message about closings due to inclement weather.

- Local safety officials can reassure citizens about a situation in the community.

- A publicist for a motion picture company can influence audience perception about a new film.

- A community organization can announce the postponement of a charity event and distribute new details.

- A consumer company can introduce a new product.

- A real estate agent can comment on the robustness of the local market to counteract media reports of a softening national trend.

- A shopping mall can deliver its own report to the local radio station about the results of a charitable community event and subtly promote the mall.

You have become part of this exciting new trend of participatory journalism. This is an element of the quickly emerging style of media relations, when providing the media with a story and the role of reporting the story come together and meet in a transparent and credible manner.

"Technology means that studios are no longer the sole preserve of the broadcasters. Whether it's politicians broadcasting from their bedrooms or financial analysts commenting live from the floor of their bank's dealing room, arguably access to airtime has never been simpler," said the BBC's Jon Williams. "You can be at your desk at work one minute and on air the next."

Eye Candy

My strategic communications agency worked with the marketing and PR people at Learjet headquarters in Wichita, Kansas, on their challenge to introduce a new business jet, the Learjet 45. Rollouts of new corporate jets had become so commonplace in Wichita that even the hometown daily newspaper, *The Wichita Eagle*, no longer saw any news value in them.

I discussed our situation with noted photographer and photojournalist Ed Lallo, whom I had hired to get publicity pictures of the new business jet. Lallo had never before worked on an aviation project and came to town with fresh ideas on how to get a winning photo of the Learjet 45. His best idea was both daring and dangerous: to get the then-Learjet CEO, Brian Barents, to stand on top of a Learjet 45 for a photo session. My job was to talk Barents into the stunt, and Barents didn't let me down.

The next morning, we were out before dawn with a dew-covered Learjet 45 on a remote tarmac of Wichita's airport with two cherry-picker cranes — one to hoist the CEO up on top of the jet, and the other to position Lallo, with all his camera gear, right above the nose of the jet.

I stood in the background, noting that Barents was wearing slick-soled Italian loafers while standing on the curved and still dew-moistened top of the jet, about 20 feet in the air. There were no safety nets, and he stayed in position only through his own nerve and calm balance.

photo by Ed Lallo

Lallo rapid-fired both of his cameras and got the picture he wanted within 60 seconds. Barents was carefully retrieved from his dangerous perch, and the photo shoot was complete. Next step: a quick trip to a local one-hour photo lab and a check of the negatives. Then on to the local Associated Press office where, through Lallo's personal contacts, a photo was scanned and transmitted to AP headquarters in New York.

From there the photo went to newspapers nationwide on the AP PhotoWire, along with a caption I wrote that began "On Top of the Industry — Brian Barents, Learjet president and CEO, feels like he's on top of the world with the rollout of the first Learjet 45, an aircraft that redefines the light jet." The caption went on to trumpet the debut of the Learjet 45 and a couple of the aircraft's special features.

Our photo with caption was picked up by more than 800 newspapers across America with a readership of 34 million people, making it one of the most successful promotions in the business of corporate aviation. And yes, one of those papers was *The Wichita Eagle*, which ran the photo in the middle of the front page, above the fold, the next morning. Overnight one imaginative photo broke the mold and set a new standard for how business aircraft were promoted through the general news media.

All of a sudden the phones at Learjet were ringing. Used to catering to corporations, the company had found the pulse of a whole new market of potential customers: wealthy individuals who could afford the price tag. These individuals, many of them software and technology *nouveau riche*, wanted an affordable jet. Yet until that time, these individuals had been an elusive audience for Learjet, because they had never before owned a business aircraft, did not read the aviation trade magazines where Learjet advertised and, consequently, the company had not figured out how to get their attention.

Our work for Learjet was such a success that we soon involved the photography genius of Ed Lallo in another event: the celebration of the merger of two railroad giants, CSX Transportation and Conrail. At the merger event in Jacksonville, Florida, a lot was going on, including a live television program distributed via satellite to all employees of the two railroads, as well as news conferences and receptions.

But it was Lallo's visual that told the story of the success of the merger for editors at wire services and on business pages across America. He got Conrail and CSX locomotives positioned nose-to-nose and then a remarkable photo of the chief executive officers of each company, hard hats and all, joining hands in a victory salute. Once again Associated Press PhotoWire carried the story, and hundreds of newspapers used it.

photo by Ed Lallo

Remember that the news media loves good photos — unusual subjects, action, the unexpected, people doing crazy things. "Eye candy" is what some news photographers and editors call great pictures. You see them all the time in *People* magazine: photos taken by skilled photographers who are always looking for appealing and clever angles to tell the story. Good photos make news.

Not everyone can hire a professional photojournalist to help promote an event. But there is another option. Today digital cameras have opened up new opportunities in media relations for all the rest of us.

With the availability of affordable digital cameras, we can take newspaper-quality photos of nearly any occasion. Pictures taken by amateurs and photography enthusiasts are used all the time by the news media.

But remember: Always shoot the highest resolution photos you can if you believe they might be used by the news media. This simple technical consideration can make all the difference. The picture resolution of most digital cameras can be manually adjusted through either the Menu or

Function settings. You will need to play around with these settings to find the highest resolution for your particular camera brand and model.

The optimum setting to get the best quality is high resolution, low compression. That means you will get the maximum resolution on your camera with the least amount of compression, which might adversely affect quality. Newspapers and other publications generally prefer photos in a high-resolution standard — 300 dpi — which is possible only when a digital camera is set to shoot at its highest possible resolution.

When you choose these settings, you will note that the number of photos you can take on a particular memory card will decrease. That is because high-resolution photos require more space on a memory card.

You can get many more low-resolution photos on a memory card, because each picture is smaller in size, and the quality is not as good. I would consider shooting low-resolution photos on my digital camera only if the sole purpose were for online use. But then what would happen if I were to snap the picture of a lifetime in low resolution? Sure, I could put it online, but I could never use it in a publication — even 4 x 6 prints probably would look fuzzy.

It is always best to take high-resolution photos with a digital camera. Incidentally you can solve everything by purchasing a larger capacity memory card and keeping your digital camera set at the highest resolution all the time. Now, you are ready to capture your own eye candy.

Let's say you are doing media relations for an event. You have put together a list of journalists and drafted a news release in advance. Then the day of the event arrives, and you get lucky by taking a digital picture that tells the whole story — a "Wow!" type of picture that people will rave about.

This photo is potentially more valuable for promoting your event than a news release or anything else. A great picture creates a lasting impression and is often preferred by editors over a news release. All you need is a photo caption — a witty two or three lines that sum up the story that the picture tells. Then get it into the hands of the media.

Remember, as it did for Learjet, one picture can change everything.

A Deskside Payoff

A deskside briefing with a reporter can be one of the best ways to generate initial interest about your company or organization. It's particularly effective because the tactic is not widely used by many public relations practitioners. If you play your cards right and if some basic rules are followed, the deskside session can lead to a good story.

The concept is to schedule an informal meeting with a reporter, get an understanding of the reporter's needs, and talk briefly about your organization or issue. The objective of a deskside briefing is to lay the groundwork for a possible future story, provide editorial direction and build a relationship. It is not to pitch a story.

Let's say that a few journalists have written about your company, product or service, but it would be a major coup to have a story appear in the *Daily Bugle*. Yes, I made up that name.

Despite numerous calls to the person you think is the correct reporter at the *Bugle*, nothing is happening with your story. It's going nowhere. Either your calls are not being returned, or the reporter has told you that while the story seems interesting, it lacks a good news angle. That's a polite way of saying the reporter perceives your outfit as no big deal and unworthy of his or her time.

The more obvious and predictable approach of pitching a story, perhaps to a reporter you've never before met, has not worked. So you need to try something else. You are under pressure to make something happen with the *Daily Bugle*. It's time for a — drum roll, please — *deskside briefing*.

Here's how it works.

The concept is to get your CEO or an executive or an expert or you before the right reporter for a brief, early-morning background meeting. The deskside is *not* billed as an interview but as a quick background briefing. Ideally you should meet the reporter informally for about 30 minutes before his or her normal work starting time, and — this is very important — keep the meeting shorter than the time you requested.

Before you make any phone calls to a newsroom, do some research about the reporter you are approaching to make certain you are calling the right one. Take a look at some of his or her recent work so you can mention it in your conversation and compliment that work. Look for areas of overlap or connection between what reporters have previously written and your potential story.

All reporters have a particular *beat*, or range of topics they cover, often defined by their personal interests. NBC's Robert Hager, for example, has covered transportation issues for years because of his interest. Thomas Friedman at *The New York Times* has become one of the country's foremost opinion-leaders on the Middle East because of his interest in the region.

Here's a case history of how a campaign of carefully planned deskside briefings helped to turn around unfavorable news coverage and improve the corporate image for RBC Centura, a bank that serves five southeastern states.

Typical of the changing financial-services landscape across America, RBC Centura had become a subsidiary of a large financial-services company headquartered in Canada. The resulting merger was creating some confusion over the bank's earnings among local financial reporters. On top of that, important business units of RBC Centura were not performing as well as before the merger, resulting in nothing but negative news coverage for several months.

Working with Capstrat, a strategic communications firm based in Raleigh, North Carolina, RBC Centura's leaders decided to deal with the situation head-on through a series of face-to-face briefing sessions with reporters and editors. It was an opportunity to meet on a personal level, answer hard questions and fully explain the bank's perspective.

Capstrat booked the appointments with journalists in each market and provided RBC Centura executives with briefing packets that included the itinerary for each day, and key messages and talking points, as well as a digest of recent stories by the journalists they would be meeting with. Capstrat also accompanied the executives to many sessions. In six weeks' time, bank executives met with nearly two dozen news outlets in North Carolina, Georgia and Florida.

The results were quick and worked to repair the bank's flagging reputation. RBC Centura's perspective — clarifying the company's performance and point of view — appeared in every major news market in the bank's footprint. Additionally the media tour resulted in Associated Press and Dow Jones wire stories and established ongoing relationships with key reporters.

Analysis of post-tour stories revealed a tangible trend toward balanced coverage. In fact year-end analysis of news coverage showed about half of the stories were positive, and nearly 37 percent fell into a neutral or balanced category.

The deskside briefings had helped to improve the bank's image and credibly recalibrate awareness among consumers.

Sometimes the way you find just the right reporter who is interested in your potential story will surprise you.

Here's another example: My strategic communications firm represented the World Cycling Championships, the annual series of bicycle races that had traditionally been held in Europe, mostly in Italy. The event was going to happen for the first time ever in the United States. No one had ever heard of it here, and our challenge was to boost advance awareness to help drive ticket sales and attendance.

Our strategy was to first develop a number of stories in major daily newspapers about the significance of the World Cycling Championships coming to America. Those newspapers stories would help to quickly build credibility for our story and attract television news coverage, because TV news decision makers traditionally want to see a story validated in print first, before they invest the resources in covering it.

Right at the top of our list was *The Washington Post*. But we couldn't find a reporter at the *Post*'s sports department who had any interest in cycling. You could talk all day with them about baseball, football and golf, but not about racing bicycles.

After some research, we found that a general assignment reporter assigned to the paper's Metro section had written a couple of stories about local bike races in the nation's capital because he was an avid cyclist himself. In fact he rode his bicycle to work.

We called the reporter and suggested a briefing about the event. He agreed to meet us at the paper early one morning, about 45 minutes before his normal starting time. That meeting resulted in not only one terrific story but continuing coverage of the event. We never asked him for a story. We just suggested a background briefing about our event.

E-mail can be a good way to snag the attention of a reporter, especially with a clever approach, said Marcus Chan at the *San Francisco Chronicle*.

"The best e-mail pitches (or more accurately, the ones I actually read) are the ones that sound like they're coming from a regular reader; they offer meaningful and specific comments to published stories, and often, it's not until the very end that I realize it's a PR pitch. But those are the ones I read."

> "The best e-mail pitches (or more accurately, the ones I actually read) are the ones that sound like they're coming from a regular reader; they offer meaningful and specific comments to published stories, and often, it's not until the very end that I realize it's a PR pitch." — Marcus Chan, technology editor, *San Francisco Chronicle*

Crafting an effective e-mail pitch that catches a reporter's attention can reach the level of ... well, of a form of art.

Being concise is key when it comes to asking a journalist to meet about a possible story idea. You must create a brief, focused, alluring and — most of all — low-key pitch in order to schedule the meeting. Once you've got the right journalist, you need to hook his interest —

the quicker the better. Your chances diminish the more you talk. Whether you send an e-mail, leave a message on voice mail or actually get the reporters on the phone live, get right to the point with an action plan. Tell them you have a possible story in mind and why you think they might be interested, briefly referencing something similar they've written. OK, I will say it: Play to their egos.

When you get the attention of the right reporter, don't waste his or her time with trivial politeness unless you are personal pals. Avoid beginning a call or e-mail with "How are you today?" or the insipid phrase "What's up?" Get right to the point.

Then do something unusual: Do not pitch a story. That's too predictable. Say something like, "This may or may not lead to a story, but I think it is important to at least give you a brief backgrounder about our organization, and here's why …"

You are not pitching a story but merely seeking a meeting to provide background. This unique approach implies exclusiveness. It merits a reporter meeting you and your boss before work to at least listen. Underscore to the reporter that you know the importance of his or her work demands and, besides, your boss has a limited amount of time as well, so an early-morning meeting would work best. Remember, it's an informal meeting.

Here are some general rules:

- It is best not to send information prior to the deskside meeting for a couple of reasons. First, it begins to feel like a predictable story pitch. Second, you may be sending the wrong material. Third, the reporter is likely to lose or misplace the stuff sent in advance, which could create an awkward moment when you arrive and the reporter can't find it. Send advance material only if the reporter specifically insists on it, and then send only what is requested — nothing more.

- Resist the traditional public relations urge to impress the reporter with reams of news media kits and a load of stuff. When you go to a deskside, intentionally take only the briefest supporting material with you — preferably no brochures, no media kit. I suggest taking only a one-page bio on the official who is meeting with the reporter. In that way you create an opportunity to have personalized follow-up contact with the reporter by providing specific material the reporter wants as a result of the meeting. That not only keeps the reporter focused on your potential story, it also works to build a relationship of trust and confidence with the reporter and boosts your chances that a story will happen.

- Make sure, in advance, that your boss understands the purpose of the deskside briefing, especially that first, it is not an interview, but a briefing; and second, you are not asking the reporter to do a story. It's an informal chance to meet — for the first time — a journalist who can be important to your organization. It is *relationship building*.

- During the meeting, focus on one or two main messages. Avoid making the reporter's eyes glaze over by talking about too many issues. Focus on a couple of competitive advantages that may complement the reporter's past articles.

- At the conclusion of a deskside briefing, define an informal follow-up plan. Ask the reporter if there is any material you can send that might be helpful. Find out the best way you can stay in touch — e-mail, phone.

- Thank the reporter for his or her time. Show sincere appreciation. And do not — ever — ask for a story. Even if the reporter suggests a possible story, say you would be happy if the conversation led to that, but you just appreciated meeting for a few minutes.

Once I took a CEO for an early-morning deskside briefing with a reporter and when the meeting concluded, the executive could not resist the urge, even though I had advised him against it, to ask, "When are you going to do a story?" The reporter understandably looked ambushed.

The deskside meeting had been scheduled with the understanding that it was neither an interview nor an implied commitment to do a story. It was a unique opportunity to meet with a reporter who had or might have otherwise said no to a traditional interview. We had broken the ground rules of the meeting. It was like breaking a promise.

On the other hand, deskside briefings can be very effective. Newspaper columnist and talk-show host Greg Dobbs told me of meeting with a public relations representative about the trend toward just-in-time manufacturing, a process of efficiently managing often costly inventories to allow more competitive pricing of products.

"She made me aware of a concept growing in popularity in American industry," Dobbs said. "When she had my attention, she then offered her client to serve as my example in a feature story. It worked. Win-Win.

"She turned me on to the concept, and then, by getting me in her client's door, earned her pay."

The *New York Post*'s Linda Stasi cautions, "We know and you know that you're there to sell something I probably don't want, so be upfront about it. Never, never oversell or lie. If you do, remember, the reporter is the one with the last word — and that word will be in ink and read (hopefully) by many people."

> Never, never oversell or lie. If you do, remember, the reporter is the one with the last word — and that word will be in ink and read (hopefully) by many people." — Linda Stasi, columnist, *New York Post*

I received an e-mail from a public relations person in the state of Qatar in the Middle East who said a deskside briefing may be ideal in a perfect situation, but his primary media contacts are far-flung around the world, making in-person meetings nearly impossible. I understand his challenge, but the objectives are to get to know a journalist at some level of familiarity, work to establish trust and build a professional relationship.

Yes, a face-to-face meeting is preferable, but the concept also will work through a telephone conversation with follow-up e-mail contact, and the same rules apply.

A deskside briefing — in whatever form it takes — is a resourceful way to get the attention of an important reporter and establish a productive working relationship that will pay off and help you get an edge on your competitors.

A Time and a Place for News Releases

News releases are an overused crutch in the public relations business. Many public relations people criticize the news media for not paying attention to their organizations but rely solely on issuing a never-ending string of poorly written news releases — which seldom have any relevance or news value and are often self-serving drivel, a holdover from a bygone era of media relations.

Brian Lamb, the founder and chief executive officer of C-SPAN, said news releases are the worst way to communicate with the media. "Public relations people," he said, "simply do not understand that the media is certainly not driven by and generally does not care about news releases."

While a news release unquestionably can get the attention of a reporter or editor, it's not often that a release by itself results in a news story, except at smaller newspapers.

From a journalist's perspective, it's fairly rare to see a news release that contains legitimate, balanced news.

Yet many public relations people — and their bosses — think that all they need to do is issue a release, and the media will come running. It doesn't work that way.

Veteran journalists generally have become wary of trivial fluff or blatantly commercial self-promotion under the "news release" banner.

"When I get a news release telling me of a new hire, or burying the lead of a plausible story," said Denver-based newspaper columnist and television journalist Greg Dobbs, "then anything else I get from them feels like too much. Knowing my priorities means, among other things, knowing when I might use their information and knowing when I might not ... which is 'when' they shouldn't send it in the first place."

> "When I get a news release telling me of a new hire, or burying the lead of a plausible story then anything else I get from them feels like too much. Knowing my priorities means, among other things, knowing when I might use their information and knowing when I might not ... which is 'when' they shouldn't send it in the first place." — Greg Dobbs, newspaper columnist and television journalist

Effective news releases must be just that — news. Not fluff, not a sales promotion, certainly not "about" your company — but legitimate news. The news release must present *a story*.

Here are just the first two paragraphs of a classic example of a jargon-laden corporate promotion announcement under the guise of a news release. This is from software developer MicroStrategy:

> McLEAN, Va., January 10, 2005 — MicroStrategy® Incorporated (NASDAQ: MSTR), a leading worldwide provider of business intelligence software, today announced that Gartner, Inc. has placed it in the visionary quadrant of both the Enterprise Business Intelligence Suites (EBIS) and BI Platform segments of Gartner Inc.'s 2004 "Magic Quadrants for Business Intelligence" report.

> "We are honored to be positioned so prominently in both the EBIS and BI Platforms Magic Quadrants," said MicroStrategy's COO Sanju Bansal, "We believe inclusion in both business intelligence quadrants highlights MicroStrategy's exceptional ability to support a complete spectrum of business users and a wide variety of reporting and analysis applications from a single, integrated architecture."

What's a visionary quadrant, and what makes it magic? Why is the news release seemingly written in code? Not only are terms not explained anywhere in the news release, but by the third paragraph, MicroStrategy® had moved on to blatantly promote two other apparently unrelated products, never returning to explain why anyone on the planet should care about a visionary quadrant or BI Platform.

In this example, a company devoted only 108 words, or just 12 percent, of a total 896-word news release to making its news announcement. The remainder was a sales pitch. By the way, it's both bad form and unnecessary in a legitimate news release for a company to use the registered trademark — ® — symbol.

George Lewis, who covers technology for NBC News, told me, "one piece of advice to PR people when pitching tech stories: tell reporters in ordinary English why the gadget or service they're promoting will make ordinary people's lives better. Don't use terms like 'comprehensive multitasking solution' because that sort of yadda-yadda-yadda makes my eyes glaze over.

"And, if you can't figure out how your product will positively impact ordinary people, don't bother pitching it. And remember, we don't do infomercials for your client. We're covering trends more than gadgets, and your client's product may be lumped in with the competition's if we do the story."

Credibility is damaged when a company unabashedly uses an alleged news release as an advertisement. In this case, MicroStrategy appeared to have used a news release as a way to promote its wares rather than buy an ad.

On the other hand, Nike Inc. defused potentially adverse news of a store closing through a timely and comprehensively written news release that appeared to candidly present the full story. They smartly addressed the problem head-on. The headline read "Nike, Inc. to Cease Operations at NikeTown Orange County."

> Beaverton, Ore. (3 January, 2005) — Today Nike, Inc. announces its plans to cease operations at NikeTown Orange County on January 30th, 2005. Opened in 1993, the store at Triangle Square Mall in Orange County was one of the first NikeTowns — the company's premiere retail space for showcasing innovative products and deepening Nike's connection to consumers. In recent years, however, the mall has experienced low tenant occupancy. As such, Nike believes that the closure of the store is in the best interest of the brand. We will continue to serve Orange County consumers

through NikeTown Los Angeles, NikeWomen stores in Orange County (Newport Beach and Costa Mesa), nike.com and existing partners at retail.

Nike will support affected employees by offering all store associates competitive severance packages, in accordance with our guidelines and California labor laws. In addition, we encourage individuals to identify opportunities that fit their experience within the Company and apply accordingly.

This news release is professionally written and reflects a major company that wants to protect its brand while supporting customers and doing something for employees who will lose their jobs. Nike, in laying out the situation with the store closing, subtly lays the blame on a shopping mall that may have some problems. The company also manages to include some cross-promotion in a classy manner.

News releases need a purpose, as in the Nike example. What are you announcing, and why is it important? Stick to one purpose, and seek to establish credibility through candor and openness.

The general idea is to use the release not to provide the whole story but to capture the media's interest and make them want to learn more about the subject or issue. How do you achieve that?

Here are some ways:

- *Take a journalist's perspective.* Is your news release actually timely news that the media might find interesting, or is it self-serving fluff? Develop a legitimate news story in the news release — something the media will find appealing.

- *Cut to the chase.* Why should anyone care? Get to the bottom line in the first sentence, then provide background in the body of the release. Isn't that how news stories are crafted by the media? They write a headline that catches your eye, then provide enough in the first sentence or two to whet your appetite. If you want to know more, read on.

- *Be timely.* This is one essential element of news. Develop timely news releases.

- *Keep the news release to one page.* You heard me: One page. I assure you that when you go beyond one page, the media's attention drops exponentially, regardless of what you have to say.

- *Give the media an easy way to contact you and learn more.* Give them your phone numbers and make sure you answer, and that it doesn't go to voicemail.

When developing a news release, remember that most releases are rarely if ever used, so be realistic and imaginative. Use news releases as working tools for journalists to provide clarity on your messages and focus for what you have to say. Good news releases can be valuable weapons in the communications arsenal.

Most of all, don't oversell. A news release is supposed to showcase credible news that you have to announce — clear, compelling and straightforward. Avoid all those overworked promotion words; they don't work in a news release except to undermine your purpose and turn off reporters.

Paper the news media too many times with promotion or sales pieces under the guise of a "news release," and you will not only kill their interest in your organization when you have something real to announce, you will drive them to your competitor.

A news release recently crossed my desk from a chain of stores called FARM♦MART. The one-page release contained the use of the company's logo — "FARM♦MART" — 14 times, exactly like that, including the diamond symbol between the words, part of their logo. Not FarmMart or Farm Mart or even FARMMART, but FARM♦MART.

Not only does such commercial branding not belong in a news release, but it hurts the credibility of the company, because the news media most likely will disregard it.

And the enormous volume of releases with trivial subject matter can have the same adverse effect. A few years ago the corporate communications department at Sprint — the telecommunications company — would issue a news release about every new hire at corporate headquarters in Overland Park, Kansas. This wasn't the result of a plan or strategic objective, just a bad habit. Some thought it was because the head of corporate communications at the time had limited experience in public relations.

The avalanche of daily news releases completely got out of hand and inundated BusinessWire, the paid news release distribution wire. Even though BusinessWire was making a bundle on all the Sprint business, the trivial nature of the releases was undermining credibility for both Sprint and BusinessWire to the point that the wire service sent a representative to Sprint headquarters to politely ask them to get a grip.

Sprint is certainly not the only company that has cranked out meaningless news releases. The practice is more often the case than the exception. Yet the news media is not driven by and generally doesn't care about news releases, to echo the words of C-SPAN's Brian Lamb.

Effective media relations is about having solid contacts among journalists and knowing how to present a story idea.

"I find that 90 percent of PR people do a really poor job," said Barbara Bradley Hagerty of National Public Radio. "They pitch stories with no angles, just kind of pitch randomly. They don't think through that journalists need a *news* peg. They don't offer specifics for sources to back up the story or how we can cover it quickly."

"Rarely is a story pitched right," according to Richard Danbury of BBC Television News in London. "I suppose a key here is to know the journalists' preoccupations and pitch accordingly. When I was a lawyer, I was taught the golden rule of advocacy: know thy tribunal."

> "Rarely is a story pitched right. I suppose a key here is to know the journalists' preoccupations and pitch accordingly." — Richard Danbury, BBC Television News

In the important tribunal of public opinion, how you are seen, perceived and talked about when you make news — or attempt to make news — can make all the difference between recognition as a winner or standing in the shadows as a runner-up. The distinctive style with which you practice media relations — the approaches you take and the words you use — will make the difference. It's all up to you.

If You Write One, Make It Good

Despite the potential shortcomings mentioned in the last chapter, news releases are a traditional and, at times, a necessary tool of media relations. It's all in how you do it. To fully take advantage of an opportunity, a news release must communicate news. Use it to give journalists a real, legitimate story.

Each day the news media is bombarded with thousands of trivial, self-serving news releases. Imagine your competitive edge if you create a news release that contains genuine news and *looks* like a news story!

With the increasing trend in the news business to downsize staffs and consolidate news operations, a news release styled after a news story has a much better chance of getting used than just another predictable news release coming across their desks.

All kinds of events can provide the opportunity for a good news release. A release to the news media can, for example:

- Announce a new product or service.
- React to a timely situation.
- Trumpet a new development at your organization.
- Provide perspective about an event.
- Attempt to present your side in an adverse situation.

Chad Campbell, producer of "The Bob Edwards Show" on XM Satellite Radio, called my attention to the cleverest news release he had ever received.

"I never pay much attention to a press release," Chad explained about how he selects topics for the program. "If the topic doesn't interest me, what the press release says won't matter much.

"There is one press release that really worked on me though. It was written by the author, Rob Walker. He poked fun at the concept of the press release and really caught my attention ... of course, it LOOKS just like a typical press release."

When I contacted Walker, he explained that he had known publicity for his book would be an uphill challenge, so he had nothing to lose by having some fun with his goofy news release which, by the way, worked to get meaningful media attention.

Walker's main headline screamed:

Is there anything less than one more idiotic Press Release?!

The content of his news release read:

Our world is already a swamp of pointless hype. And something about the press release for yet 'ANOTHER!' new book is particularly monotonous. All such documents look the same: perfunctory and ephemeral. It's as if the people who write and design them know that they are wasting everyone's time, including their own. Still, there is a formula, and I will follow it. Yes, it's a new book. It's called 'Letters From New Orleans.'

Hey, so, you know, maybe you should write about this book and tell people to buy it, how does that sound? Invite me on your show, post about the book on your blog, or just tell all your friends. Oh: I'm available for interviews! You can ask me if I'm guilty of doing exactly the same thing that I'm pretending to criticize.

An outrageous approach to a news release, you say? Unprofessional? Downright wacko? Maybe, maybe not. Walker got more media coverage than he expected and has sold some books along the way. For him it worked.

People ask me at the media relations workshops I conduct to show them an example or two of a really terrific news release, and I always hesitate. I'll do the same here because what I want to write is a book that sparks your creative imagination and curiosity to explore new tactics and understand new trends for media relations that I have learned from interviewing many journalists, as opposed to providing another how-to guide on writing a news release.

If you still need some examples, check out Nike's Web site. They do a good job. Better yet, learn how to write a real, honest-to-goodness news story in the same style that you see in your local newspaper. That's what reporters want from you: a story. Write a news release like a reporter writes a front-page story.

That said, I will share basic guidelines for an effective news release. The creative and imaginative approach to content is up to you. Always begin by thinking of your audience first, and that includes reporters and editors, the gatekeepers to your audiences through media channels.

Even such a typically mundane news release as one that announces a new hire or promotion within your organization can be meaningful if you consider how the hire or promotion enhances value or provides a service to your key audiences. A new-hire news release might read something like this: "As XYZ Company increases emphasis on customer service, the company announces that Mary Smith has accepted the position of vice president of customer satisfaction …"

To help you focus on its news content, imagine how your news release might appear if it were run verbatim in the newspaper as actual news. In real life, of course, that rarely happens — although some PR people claim otherwise.

Here are examples of four basic types of news releases, although the lines between them sometimes blur:

- *Announcement.* This is a common kind of news release used to announce such events as new products or services; new employees; promotions; reports about sales, earnings, mergers and financials; openings and closings; expansion and construction of facilities; layoffs and employment opportunities.

- *Spot or timely announcement.* This type of news release often announces an upcoming event or occurrence. It can be driven by outside occurrences over which you may have no control, such as a natural disaster, inclement weather or terrorism. A spot announcement is used to provide timely information updates to the news media.

- *Controlled-message announcement.* This is the type of news release organizations use to try to suppress bad news and get across their message in an adverse environment. This kind of news release usually makes matters worse because an organization is perceived — often accurately — as hiding behind the release rather than engaging in a healthy interaction with the news media.

- *Reaction release.* A reaction news release is generally used in a time-critical situation when it is important to comment on something that affects an organization, such as new legislation or a lawsuit. It is also used to provide an organization's position on some timely outside occurrence that has some bearing on the organization. For example if a federal agency has announced new guidelines for the industry in which your company does business, a reaction release can help position your organization as a leader.

Begin by getting in a news frame of mind. Sit down and actually read today's newspaper. Don't go online, but rather go out and pick up a copy of today's paper. It's only in that way that you will get an authentic feel for stories. Look at how headlines are written and pay special attention to how the first paragraph or two of each story is written. You want to clone that style of writing in a news release.

Next plan your news release. Here are some steps to follow each and every time you have a news release to draft. First ask yourself these questions:

- *What's the purpose?* Why are you doing a news release? In many cases, it's because the boss thought it was a good idea or the "suits" in the front office cooked up some new sales promotion, and they're hoping a news release will get them results without the expense of buying ads. If your reasons fit into those categories, that's not good enough. Sure, a news release can legitimately and credibly announce a new sales promotion, but it can never drive sales. *It is essential to establish a clear and focused news purpose for the news release.*

- *Is your news newsworthy?* The purpose of a news release is to inform a public audience through the news media of your news item. Do not use your news release to try to make a sale. A good news release answers all of the W questions (who, what, where, when and why), providing the media with useful information about your organization, product, service or event. *If you read your news release, and it reads like an advertisement, rewrite it.*

- *Who is it designed to reach, and why should they care?* A news release is not a place to dance around the central point. Your message goes hand in hand with the purpose, and you must get to the point right away. Vaguely defined news releases, lacking purpose, are one of the biggest irritants to the journalists who receive them. There might be actual news hidden in there somewhere, but it takes too long to find. *Remember that most news releases are reviewed in just a split second by someone in a newsroom due to the volume received every day.*

- *What is in it for this particular audience?* What are the potential values or the benefits or rewards to a public audience? *Again, consider these factors from an outsider's perspective.*

- *What is the goal of your organization in issuing a news release?* Is there a call to action? A timely event that you want people to attend? A new product hitting the market that will make life easier? *Create a news release that contains legitimate and timely news. That's how to get your story in the news media.*

Some other points to remember:

- *Be timely.* One of the best ways to get the media to pay attention to your news release is to make it timely. You can get a reporter's attention by providing the scoop on a news story that's about to happen. You can enhance the appeal, if possible, by explaining how your news release is relevant to other timely and important news. For example if you are announcing a healthy lifestyles fair at a local shopping mall in a news release and you notice that there have been a number of stories on television and in the newspapers about obesity, look for a way to position your event as a solution to that problem.

- *Write for the news media.* Journalists will commonly use a news release as a springboard for a larger feature story. Try to develop a story as you would like to have it told. Even if your news is not reprinted verbatim, it may provide an acceptable amount of exposure.

- *Stick to the facts.* Tell the truth. Avoid fluff, embellishments and exaggerations. If you feel that your news release contains embellishments, perhaps it would be a good idea to set it aside until you have more exciting news to share. If you get outside the facts, remember you might be risking your organization's credibility, reputation and brand. It never hurts to tone it down a bit.

- *Use an active voice.* A passive voice is bland. Verbs in the active voice help to bring your news release to life. A tip here for fine-tuning skills is to review Strunk and White's *The Elements of Style*. It is the classic and essential reference book on the rules of usage and principles of composition most commonly violated.

- *Use the present tense.* Avoid writing that "the company announced." Such use of past tense is to report history. Instead, write your news release in an active, more engaging voice.

- *Beware of jargon.* While a limited amount of jargon will be required if your goal is to optimize your news release for online search engines, the best way to communicate your news is to speak plainly, using ordinary language. Jargon is language specific to certain professions or groups and is not appropriate for general readership. Avoid such terms as *capacity planning techniques, extrapolate* and *prioritized evaluative procedures*.

- *Avoid hype.* The exclamation point — ! — will kill your credibility with the media. Using **bold text** does not make your release more important.

A news release should be well-written and follow a basic, clean format. Good margins, double-spaced lines, short paragraphs and meaningful quotes make it easy to read.

Follow a standard format that can subtly help brand the image of your organization, but keep in mind that a news release is not an advertisement. A release should follow a style that makes it look like a story, within a format that the media recognizes. Remember, a news release is like telling a story, but you must get to the point of the story in the first sentence.

Here are some formatting rules for news releases:

- Double-space your text.
- Use a standard serif font, such as Times New Roman or Palatino, in 11- or 12-point type.
- As a general rule, there is no need to indent each paragraph; rather double-space between paragraphs.
- Try to keep a news release to one page. If it must be longer, number the pages.
- Write "more" at the end of each page if the release continues.
- Use the familiar journalistic symbol "###" at the end of your release.

Here is a summary of the elements of a news release, based on the Associated Press style for news releases preferred by most newspapers:

<u>For Immediate Release</u>. Underline it. Bold it, if you wish, and left-justify it at the top of your page. That signals the media that you have something to say right now. Never, ever use the phrase *advance for release*. That was in style a decade or so ago and is perceived by the media as manipulative. There's nothing to be gained by saying "Here's something so hot that you cannot use it now, but I wanted to let you in on it early …"

Date. That's the day of the week and date of your release. For example, "Tuesday, March 2, 2005." The day and date go right under <u>For Immediate Release</u>. Using both day and date is a good practice. Despite all our best intentions, we sometimes make mistakes on dates alone. And there's an old jinx that says when you put just the date with no day, two times out of four, it'll be wrong. Go figure.

Headline. Write a headline for your news release that looks like one right out of *USA Today*. *USA Today* is a good newspaper to pattern after because their headlines are often catchy and seductive. For example, AARP created a promotion under the banner: "Gray & Glamorous: AARP's Golden Girls" about seven actresses, age 56 to over 70, who are considered among "Hollywood's hottest." It got them coverage everywhere, including *USA Today*.

Location. This is a city or place. For example:
(Alexandria, VA) The lead sentence starts here …

The lead paragraph. The lead is the most important part of any news release. If you think about a *pyramid* style of writing a news release, the lead is the top point, the apex. Get to the point in your lead. This is your best chance to capture a journalist's attention. In just a couple of sentences, you must give the reader basic yet compelling details of the story. So get right to the point of why anyone should care about your news. Keep the lead paragraph short — two to three short sentences maximum, and no more than about four or five lines.

Body of text. The body of text contains several paragraphs that provide broader details. Visualize the pyramid getting wider as we grow it with more supporting information, including facts, supporting information and relevant quotes.

Summary. Wrap up your news release by pulling together the importance of what you have announced in the lead and body of text. Repeat, if necessary, and underscore the timeliness and relevance of your news announcement. This is the base of the pyramid.

I use this pyramid example to contrast the style of many news releases that are sent to newsrooms, written like *inverted pyramids* — too fat and and too wordy in the lead paragraph. I know that my pyramid example runs counter to the pyramid style taught in journalism school, but I use it here to illustrate that the lead paragraph of a news release must immediately *get to the point* in a few words or it will just end up in the discard pile.

By the way, it is OK to use your organization's letterhead. There's no compelling benefit in having a special news release letterhead.

While it is nearly impossible and certainly not particularly smart to suggest a hard-and-fast set of rules for a news release, there are four basic paragraphs or components of an effective release. These components constitute the inverted-pyramid approach to writing a news release:

Paragraph 1: Most important facts of the release. This is the attention grabber. Get right to the point of the news release immediately.

Paragraph 2: Essential background material and the names of key characters or sources.

Paragraph 3: Elaboration on material contained in the first paragraph plus additional background information.

Paragraph 4: Concise summary of the news in the release.

Contact: At the end of the news release, include the contact person's full name, office and cell phone numbers and e-mail address. Here is an example:

Contact: Heinie Manush
            Office: (703) 555-1212
            Cell: (202) 555-2323
            E-mail: BaseballRules@heiniemanush.com

I highly recommend two books by The Associated Press to learn more about the style of news releases that journalists prefer: *The Associated Press Stylebook* and *The Associated Press Guide to Punctuation.* They are today's bibles for style in journalism and public relations, and copies are available at most bookstores.

Ultimately, though, all the structure and format in the world won't save you without good content — what you have to say. Use the news release format to tell a timely and relevant story — a story that is compelling, interesting and that informs, motivates and excites the news media to immediately form a good opinion of your organization. Use it as a door opener, an appetizer to journalists, to develop good coverage and make news.

Forget Lists, Find Influencers

There's a popular misconception in the public relations industry that the larger the media list — the more names on it — the better. During my public relations agency years I've found this to be particularly characteristic of corporate communications departments in large companies. Quantity over quality is the conventional wisdom.

In fact an entire cottage industry of service companies that offer media lists has sprung up. Thousands and thousands of names are provided. The series of *Bacon's Media Directories*, for example, has gotten so thick and heavy that it's hard just to lift the books onto your desk. Bacon's and other services, like *Burrelle's Media Directory*, are also available online in a user-friendly and much lighter format.

Vocus, another one of the numerous online services that provide media relations support, boasts "access to a global media directory of over 400,000 unique journalists, updated daily." Holy cow! Am I impressed? Certainly not.

Unquestionably, these services deliver valuable and specific contact information about people in the news media, but are all those names really needed by your organization? And are they worth the expense? The answer is no.

Today's style of media relations involves narrowing your focus and resources to the areas in which you will have the maximum impact. That means reducing your media list and concentrating on those reporters who can best cover your organization.

Jennifer Barrett of *Newsweek* spoke for most journalists when she said, "It would be more effective for a PR person to concentrate their efforts on a couple dozen key reporters and get to know what topics they like and what they tend to write about most, and build trust with them, rather than to spend their time sending out dozens of generic e-mails to reporters and hoping someone bites.

> "It would be more effective for a PR person to concentrate their efforts on a couple dozen key reporters and get to know what topics they like and what they tend to write about most, and build trust with them, rather than to spend their time sending out dozens of generic e-mails to reporters and hoping someone bites." — Jennifer Barrett, associate editor, *Newsweek*

"When I'm in a crunch, I go first to those PR people whom I trust and I know I can rely on to get the right sources quickly. I literally have a short list of about a half-dozen PR people to whom I turn regularly for story sources."

Barrett's advice is brilliant for people who are responsible for media relations: Become a trusted media source. Build relationships with journalists, as you have heard many times in this book, and become a credible source.

Roy Gutman, *Newsday*'s foreign editor who won the Pulitzer Prize for investigative reporting, concurs. "Be the database for the issue you support, and don't seek credit, even for a job well done.

"If you have a genuine story," Gutman shared with me, "openness, readiness to connect a reporter with the authentic voices of the story and general assistance is truly welcome."

Using a shotgun approach to media relations by sending news releases and stories randomly to as many reporters and news organizations as possible seldom works, can cost a ton of money and often tends to hurt your reputation rather than help it. It doesn't work.

It's always important to maintain an up-to-date list of media contacts, but quality of contacts is far more important than quantity. Many public relations people are insecure and concerned they might miss sending something to someone important in the news media, but it's not necessary to pepper a whole newsroom with your releases.

The news media is inundated every day by too much publicity stuff that's too poorly targeted. In some cases the same media materials are sent to multiple reporters and editors, regardless of whether they cover the issue or not. Some of it is sent to reporters at organizations for which they haven't worked for years. In yet other cases the right reporter doesn't receive a copy.

An important element of effective media relations is targeting the right journalists with a story angle that might capture their interest.

The single most valuable piece of advice offered by Scott Simon, host on National Public Radio, is "Know who you are calling. I am amazed at the number of calls I get from people representing books (like *100 Ways to Grow a Great Rutabaga!*), CDs or people that no one who listens to our program should think we would be interested in. We don't keep our show a secret; several million people listen. Before you call us, you should try to put yourself among them, at least for a week or two, to make a better informed presentation."

> "Know who you are calling. I am amazed at the number of calls I get from people representing books (like *100 Ways to Grow a Great Rutabaga!*), CDs or people that no one who listens to our program should think we would be interested in. We don't keep our show a secret; several million people listen. Before you call us, you should try to put yourself among them, at least for a week or two, to make a better informed presentation." — Scott Simon, correspondent, National Public Radio

So how do you start crafting a media list that will achieve results?

Stop for a minute and think about the number of reporters who have written anything about your organization or business in the last year. You will generally find that this is no more than a handful.

Of course if you work for a high-profile company with many consumer products and services — such as Microsoft, Coca-Cola, GE or Colgate — it may be a different story. But even then it is likely that only a few reporters follow your outfit on a regular basis and do the substantive reporting that influences other journalists.

As senior vice president for the corporate image and reputation management practice at Edelman Public Relations, I encountered the head of communications for a major aerospace company who had never bothered, in several years on the job, to learn the name of one single reporter who covered his company. He told me, flatly, that he hired us to deal with the news media because he didn't want to be bothered. Such an attitude is blatantly irresponsible, and it's not surprising that the fellow subsequently lost his job.

When it came right down to it we found that only about eight or 10 journalists covered the aerospace company on a regular basis, and what they reported carried broad influence throughout the aerospace industry and even to Wall Street.

I'd be willing to bet that for most corporations, there are fewer than a dozen reporters who really count when it comes to getting out a story about the organization, and it is the job of the person in charge of media relations to establish and skillfully nurture relationships with these reporters.

And while you are making contacts with reporters and editors, don't overlook the wire services. The stories written by reporters at The Associated Press, Reuters and Bloomberg appear in hundreds of newspapers. Those reporters are the *media influencers.* They set the tone for others, and they are critical to your organization. Find them and court them. Communicate with them personally on a regular basis, never through an intermediary service. Get to know them and what they need and seek in story ideas.

Here's a checklist for creating an effective top-tier media list:

- *Get online and find out who writes about your organization.* Use an online news retrieval service, such as ProQuest or LexisNexis, to find the newspaper and magazine stories written about your organization in the last year. These archiving services provide access, usually with a nominal charge, to thousands of current periodicals and newspapers, many updated daily and containing full-text articles that date back to the mid- to late 1980s. You want to find stories in which a reporter invested some time and wrote a substantial piece of journalism about your organization or business arena. Make a list of those reporters and pay particular attention to the ones who have written thoughtful pieces about your company. Put them at the top of the list.

- *Invest in resource materials.* If your budget will allow it, consider the services of a respected news media contact service, such as Bacon's or Burrelle's. They will provide the basic information about specific media, reporters, beats and contact information. But don't let them do your job for you. The news business is transient. Reporters move around a lot, either within their company or between news organizations. Consequently there's a chance that today's accurate media contact information will be outdated tomorrow.

- *Make phone calls.* Get the latest and most accurate media contact information. Reach out to news organizations that are important to you. If your online research hasn't turned up good results, no problem. Simply make a list of media that you believe might be interested in reporting your story or, more important, where you would like to see your story appear, and give them a call. Let's say, for example, that you work for a not-for-profit group that develops after-school programs to help urban youth, and you want to generate media coverage in cities like Philadelphia, Boston and Atlanta. It's easy. Begin by calling the metro or local news assignment desks of the local media in those cities. Ask who covers education or inner-city issues and speak with that reporter. Most journalists are eager to know of an interesting new story. A phone call to a news organization often leads to the most valuable kind of contact. That's a key step in getting ready for a story pitch to the media.

- *Test the water.* If in doubt about whether you have a news story, ask when you call a news organization for updated contact details. There is nothing wrong with calling a reporter whom you have identified as being interested in your organization and saying, "I think I've got the elements of a good story for you, but I need a little help giving it focus." You will be surprised at the helpful guidance you will receive.

- *Keep it professional.* Find out how they prefer to be contacted about future news from your business and get all their contact details. Remember, it's not a conversation. Effective media relations is a ritual. You have called the reporters to plant the seeds of initial interest and ask them how they wanted to be contacted about stories. Your goal is to present a story idea in such a seductive way as to elicit a response from the journalist to learn more.

- *Update.* Even the most effective media lists don't last forever. Reporters change jobs and assignments. Make it a practice to update your entire media list at least every quarter. It's easy to do because of the contact information you've collected. If someone doesn't respond, give him or her a call. If there's still no response, assume there's been a change, and call that department at the newspaper to make inquiries and gather fresh contact details. In my media relations consulting practice, in which I work with numerous reporters all the time, I routinely get e-mails from journalists who are changing jobs or assignments.

"If there is one piece of advice I'd give PR people," said Jon Ashworth, business columnist with *The Times* of London, "it would be: 'Think before you ring.'

"It's amazing how many people call up right on deadline with some inane query or story proposal. It doesn't take a genius to figure out that you don't ring a journalist between 4 p.m. and 7 p.m. other than in response to a story of the day. I find that 11 to 12 is a good time, since journalists are between the morning news meeting and lunch. Also, work out who you are calling: I work for the daily *Times* and get calls for the *Sunday Times*." In London, the daily *Times* and *The Sunday Times* are two different news organizations.

> "It's amazing how many people call up right on deadline with some inane query or story proposal. It doesn't take a genius to

figure out that you don't ring a journalist between 4 p.m. and 7 p.m. other than in response to a story of the day. I find that 11 to 12 is a good time, since journalists are between the morning news meeting and lunch. Also, work out who you are calling: I work for the daily *Times* and get calls for the *Sunday Times*." — Jon Ashworth, columnist, *The Times* of London

Effective relationships with the news media are not something to take casually or pass along to a third party, such as a public relations agency, unless you are absolutely assured that contacts will be professionally managed.

National Public Radio's Barbara Bradley Hagerty counsels PR professionals to "figure out who you should get in touch with and go to that person directly. Work with that right person as opposed to contacting everyone. That's annoying."

The best and most responsible media coverage is usually the result of developing an ongoing professional relationship with a journalist who is interested in your story.

Again, influential media relations is all about *relationships*, which engender trust, respect and integrity.

"The best public relations people," according to Richard Serrano, Washington correspondent for the *Los Angeles Times*, "are those who are honest and forthright with information, who are willing to steer you to the right aspect of a story without compromising their side. The worst are those who refuse to comment or cooperate, and end up actually hurting their client."

Remember, it doesn't require all that much time or expense to create and maintain a great media list, because the most valuable list need not be lengthy, but rather focused, accurate and updated regularly.

You Gotta Love News/Talk Radio

News/talk radio stations, usually on the AM band, are popular from New York to Little Rock, Wilmington to Sacramento. There are hundreds of stations, many of them on the air 24 hours a day.

One of the most colorful of them is WQSV — AM 790 in Ashland City, Tennessee. Run by an equally colorful radio veteran named Corky Albright, the station is like something right out of *Northern Exposure,* a quirky television program of the late 1980s. The door is always open, and the microphone is always available to just about anyone in the community who has something to share. America needs more radio stations like WQSV.

News/talk radio is an excellent way of reaching wide audiences to talk about your organization and is a media environment where you can present a controlled message that gives people a better understanding. Talk radio stations have a lot of time on the air to fill and a big appetite for interview guests, especially if they are informative and entertaining. If you are a hit, chances are you will be asked to return.

Phil Knight, the founder of Nike, at first was a little reluctant when Edelman Public Relations booked him for an interview with Jim Bohannon, host of "The Jim Bohannon Radio Show" on Mutual and Westwood One Radio Networks, a few years ago. But when it was over, Knight said it was one of the best interview opportunities ever. Bohannon asked logical questions, and Knight was allowed to talk about the dream he turned into a $12 billion athletic shoe and clothing company. Bohannon's program is carried live on more than 300 stations nationwide.

Whether for an hour or three minutes, news/talk radio provides a forum for you to reach out and speak to new and existing audiences. Radio gives you the opportunity to casually mention the positioning message that differentiates your organization from competitors.

OK, you are convinced that news/talk radio is a good media relations tactic. How do you begin to schedule interviews?

The online service NewsLink — newslink.org — provides one of the more comprehensive lists of news/talk radio stations in the United States. And a full listing of NPR stations is available at www.npr.org. Many NPR stations feature live interview programs, usually in the midmorning. Keep in mind that the booking producers often plan several weeks and sometimes months, in advance on each program.

As with creating a media list, it's important to do initial homework to identify the programs that might best showcase your interview subject.

The easiest way is to create a media spreadsheet that includes city, radio station, programs, names of producers and contact information. Keep in mind that some news/talk stations might run feature programs at one time of the day and sports talk programs at another time. A quick phone call to the station will help guide you to the right program. You will also be able to determine the general length of interview they prefer and whether they will interview guests by telephone or insist that guests be in their studio.

By the way, never call either the general manager or the station manager, but rather ask to speak with a show producer. Deal with the people who get the programs on the air. They are the gatekeepers.

When you are satisfied with your list begin making calls approximately one month before the time you hope to book the interview. NPR stations generally plan a month in advance. Some news/talk stations plan only a couple of weeks out.

A big factor that will influence when an interview is scheduled is the timeliness of your interview. Is it tied to a holiday or event? Is it seasonal? Remember that the news media embraces timely news angles and interviews.

Make your bid for a radio interview concise and compelling. Once you identify the program you want to be interviewed on, work to get the producer on the telephone. It may require a few calls.

Explain briefly what's special about the interview you propose and why it might be of interest to the show's audience. Suggest a possible date and, if possible, a reason for seeking that date. Remember, attempt to make it a timely interview subject, such as back to school, an anniversary, an event, a time of year or whatever. A timely angle will help convince a producer to book the interview.

Once you have a yes from the producer for an interview, suggest possible background material that you can provide. Keep it brief, such as a bio on the person to be interviewed, a one-page informative fact sheet and a list of possible questions. Avoid drowning radio producers with material unless they ask for it.

Producers of current-affairs programs seek guests who have an interesting and timely story to tell that will relate to topics or news of the day and connect with their audiences. Take some time and check it out yourself. Tune in to an interview program on your local NPR station or listen to NPR's "Talk of the Nation" show that airs weekday afternoons. If evenings are better for your schedule, listen to "The Jim Bohannon Show" on Westwood One radio stations across the country.

The benefits of being interviewed on talk radio programs are significant. When the microphone is on, the door is open to say what you have to say, weave in marketing messages, deliver a compelling story, bring what you have to say *to life* with a personal anecdote, get a broad audience of listeners interested and leave a favorable impression. It's a terrific way to get immediate media exposure.

Be Clever but Not Too Clever

I knew a public relations person in Denver who felt the only way to get the media's attention was to do something flashy. So when sending out a news release she would also fill the envelope with glittery confetti — you know, the metallic stuff that's impossible to vacuum up from a carpet. I suppose she didn't feel that the content of her releases could stand up alone, so she wanted to make sure her mailings were noticed.

They were noticed all right: After making the mistake of opening her confetti-filled envelopes a couple of times, reporters and editors just pitched the whole thing, unopened, into the nearest trash can. Rather than gaining recognition as a credible public relations person, she developed a reputation as a prankster.

Everyone, including journalists, enjoy imaginative new ideas that get their attention. But if your idea only distracts the recipients, or annoys them by filling their carpets with confetti, you've lost the battle.

Unfortunately, in the public relations business, which should be distinguished by clever thinking, imaginative new ideas are few and far between. The business is instead driven by the same worn-out tactics over and over ... and over.

There is nothing wrong with trying to get the media's attention through a small gift so long as it's relevant to the story and not something expensive or valuable that might compromise a journalist's integrity or get them in hot water with their company's rules about accepting gifts. It's easy enough to find out what those rules are by making a few phone calls to reporters who cover your organization.

On the other hand, there are exceptions or gray areas, I suppose, in a journalists accepting gifts during the course of doing a story. The story about the CBS "60 Minutes" news program and Washington, D.C., philanthropist Catherine Reynolds is an example that jumps out.

"60 Minutes" decided to do a story about Reynolds, who had been the target of numerous local newspaper stories about her fight with the Smithsonian Institution. She admits she had "caused some controversy in the musty, stodgy gentlemen's club of philanthropy."

Reynolds created a fortune by turning around a failing student loan company. Then, as the head of the philanthropic Catherine B. Reynolds Foundation, she gave away millions of dollars to charities and the arts. A few years ago, Reynolds offered $38 million to the Smithsonian Institution, but when she and the Smithsonian couldn't agree on how the money would be spent, she withdrew the gift and turned her generosity toward the Kennedy Center in Washington.

So Mike Wallace and a "60 Minutes" camera crew decided to follow Ms. Reynolds around for a few days and find out something about this new benefactor on the Washington scene and what she was up to. Following her around included accompanying her on a trip to Europe aboard a luxury corporate jet she had hired.

There are still some unanswered questions about whether she and her husband would have flown in such lavish style had Wallace and his crew not been along. You and I can only draw our own conclusions. But they did, and it was first-class treatment from Reynolds and her husband all the way to London aboard a Gulfstream IV jet for Wallace, his producer, his camera crew and a couple of public relations consultants.

And just to make sure everyone had a good time, the CBS News folks were presented with digital cameras as a gift.

At this point you might be wondering what kind of story the occasionally sharp-elbowed Wallace, famous for his "ambush" style of TV news, did on Reynolds. Well, it was an extremely favorable feature, and nothing like all the other stories written about her. In fact the two of them got along "fabulously," as someone close to the story shared with me, and it showed on the air.

Prior to agreeing to do the story with "60 Minutes," Reynolds had hired a major public relations agency to frame just the right story angle, feeling and environment to win over and control "60 Minutes" coverage, and it worked.

Knowing Wallace's once-edgy type of reporting had softened in his senior years, the public relations experts did their homework. They skillfully crafted an approach that would play to his interest in helping the underdog.

Coached and briefed, Reynolds appeared to Wallace as a successful businesswoman — which she was — who had been unfairly harassed by old guard society when she was just a generous philanthropist who wanted to help improve some of America's most respected cultural institutions. It was that story that appeared on "60 Minutes," and the string of negative stories in the local media ended after such powerful national exposure.

Riding on the Gulfstream and receiving the cameras didn't hurt the news crew's opinion of Reynolds. After all, CBS could have said no to the gifts and royal treatment, in keeping with long-standing corporate policy. A former CBS News correspondent in Washington told me they should have responded "Hell, no!" to the gifts.

On the other hand, the luxury is OK with their bosses if a news crew can make a ride on a private jet part of the story — for example, shooting a little video of Reynolds while in the air en route to London.

Flying the media to Europe aboard private jets and digital cameras aside, more appropriate, affordable and realistic gifts to the media may present a challenge that can rival the creative thought you invest in developing an imaginative story pitch and supporting background materials in the first place. I have seen some public relations agencies actually spend more time trying to figure out what gifts to get than on the messages and image they hope to see in print. In the end, too many such gifts are a waste of time and money. I would call them the "predictable" gifts.

On one occasion, while I was visiting a local television news producer, he sardonically asked if I needed any oil rags for my car. At first, I wasn't sure what he meant until he pointed to a pile of T-shirts, all with a promotional message for this or that event or product. They'd been sent along with media kits and news releases by PR people. What struck me was that all the T-shirts were white and emblazoned in HUGE print in the cheapest sort of way. Certainly they were not something anyone would wear.

My friend, the producer, commented that some people in the newsroom jokingly maintained hope that someday, a really nice T-shirt might arrive that someone might not be embarrassed to wear — but hopes were fading. What was happening was the reverse of good media relations: The arrival each day of more and more T-shirts eroded more and more of the news staff's confidence in the credibility of the senders. The message was lost.

Some public relations person's "clever idea" of trying to get the media's attention by sending a T-shirt along with the news release was backfiring.

PR stunts are also fraught with hazard. There was an infamous incident in the mid-1990s when cardboard boxes with air holes in them started turning up at newspaper offices all over London. The journalists to whom they were addressed opened them to find live pigeons inside — a PR stunt designed to draw attention to a new investment product. The parcel came with instructions to release the pigeons outside.

The stunt backfired spectacularly — the animal-rights lobbyists went on the warpath — and the PR agency that cooked up the stunt lost the account.

The technology industry has been among the most ineffective in handling media relations, largely because of the limited scope of experience and creativity among the young people doing PR in that business. Despite all the useful new ideas in technology, the industry as a whole does a pretty unimaginative job when it comes to promoting itself, most often copying some old idea or something a competitor is trying.

Not only is the tech industry T-shirt crazy, but if I've seen one "stress ball" or coffee mug imprinted with the name of a tech outfit, I've seen a hundred of them.

MicroStrategy, once a technology high-flyer and known for giving out stress balls and coffee mugs to reporters, tried a slightly different approach and handed out samples of their information technology product on a compact disc for journalists. When inserted into a computer, however, the CD caused the computer to crash and resulted in corrupted files and damage that required hours to correct. Imagine the aggravation to a reporter who had relied on the computer to finish a story. A marketing person at MicroStrategy apologetically said that there had been a "glitch" in the software for the media. No kidding.

Speaking of quality, Subaru, the Japanese carmaker, once gave reporters clever-looking rollerball pens. Heck, every reporter needs another writing instrument. Problem was that the pens would bulge up and leak ink under the normal pressure of a commercial airliner. Sometimes those leaking pens were in someone's shirt pocket.

More than just a bad idea in media relations, few of these trash-and-trinket approaches have any relevance to the message a company or organization is promoting. For the media, which sees and experiences story bombardments from all directions, these approaches often only further erode credibility. Such stuff is generally thrown away, along with the "press" kits.

There are people, however, whom I would consider masters of the universe when it comes to stunts and stuff that captures valuable and influential media attention.

Many reporters in New York still remember Sir Richard Branson arriving in Times Square atop an Army tank to promote his new Virgin Cola — an event that happened years ago and is better remembered than his cola, which flopped! The tank signified challenging the competition and moving into new territory. Guess where the photo event took place? Right in front of Branson's Virgin Records store in Manhattan. Talk about brilliant cross-promoting of a brand!

It all worked together. Everything the Virgin Group used to promote the event was relevant to the occasion. Everything was first-class. The event was bold almost to the point of being outrageous, but of course, it was in New York, right?

When I was head of corporate communications at Gulfstream Aerospace, I always questioned the relevance and purpose of promotional materials that we gave to the news media. I never wanted to distract from a pitch by sending anything other than background material that was focused on getting the story — no extraneous gifts or trinkets that might possibly derail our goal of getting a story.

I had the ultimate promotional tool at my disposal that no one else on earth had ... not even Sir Richard Branson. I had an ultra long-range Gulfstream V business jet, an aircraft that could fly higher — 50,000 feet — and farther — 6,500 nautical miles — than most other aircraft in service. It is the most elegant and certainly the sexiest business jet in the sky, a symbol of achievement and success. My responsibility was to introduce the Gulfstream V to the world and build prominent visibility to attract customers.

Gulfstream, like other business aircraft manufacturers, had previously promoted its planes in the aviation trade publications and had, as a result, gotten lost in all the competitive clutter. They had for years sent out news releases and press kits to the trades, just as everyone else was doing, and it had not moved the needle toward generating widespread media coverage. Gulfstream had never considered that the mainstream media might consider their story to be appealing, and so they had not tried.

I took a completely different approach and did something unheard of in the aircraft business. Corporate CEOs and wealthy individuals, the people who can afford to buy a $40 million Gulfstream V, don't read aviation trades. They read the mainstream media. I took the Gulfstream V mainstream, to where the customers are, and it worked like a charm.

Snagging front-page coverage in papers from Los Angeles to Brussels to Beijing to Johannesburg required a lot of free rides for a lot of reporters. And what a perk it was! When I took the first Gulfstream V aircraft on world demo tours, I would contact feature and business reporters in advance for major stories to alert them that the Gulfstream V was coming to their town. At first, their reaction was "So what?"

Then I would offer a brief flight that would take them up to an altitude of 50,000 feet, above all other aircraft traffic, where the sky is nearly cobalt blue and you can clearly see the curvature of the earth. No one declined. Then I would say that the only catch was that I hoped they would write at least part of their story while at 50,000 feet. Everyone agreed.

To contrast the exclusivity of riding aboard a Gulfstream V, I kept it simple by giving each reporter who flew with us up to 50,000 feet a top-quality pilot's flight cap, embroidered "Gulfstream V — World Tour." Was it an imaginative idea? Well, I've seen better. Was it relative to the event? You bet! Only those people who flew on the aircraft got a cap. I know of some journalists who, years later, still covet those hats, because they can still boast of flying in a GV to an altitude of 50,000, nearly the edge of space. It was simple and classy and relevant, and it worked.

When I pitched a *BusinessWeek* correspondent on doing a cover story about Theodore Forstmann, the investor who owned Gulfstream at the time, the part of the deal that clinched the story was a commitment to shuttle the reporter around on a Gulfstream as he gathered background for his story. Forget the flight cap — the rides worked. We got a terrific cover story.

The rules and boundaries for a journalist accepting a gift are defined and self-imposed by each news organization. It's not determined by government regulations or mandated by industry rules. Most professional news organizations have established clear policies for their employees that set limits on what constitutes a token gift and what is bribery or payola — and therefore forbidden. The rules vary from one news organization to another. So if you have a question about gift giving, don't assume. It's always best to ask first and avoid a possible awkward situation with a journalist.

There's nothing wrong with using *trash and trinkets* — within ethical limits — to drive home a promotional message as long as the campaign is imaginative, savvy and, most of all, relevant to the story. Sometimes, you might get lucky and offer a special perk or exclusive benefit that can be experienced by the media in the course of covering your story. You will be surprised by how often that results in favorable media coverage.

It's Not Rocket Science

You have compiled a strong list of media contacts and drafted some background materials. Now it's time to make the first call to pitch your story. It's time to be imaginative and quick-witted. But what do you say? Where do you begin?

Because there are more possible options and variables in presenting a story to the news media than there are colors in the rainbow, it's probably best to just listen to what journalists say.

"The phrase 'this would be perfect for you' is one to make me wary," advised National Public Radio's Scott Simon.

Michael Rosenbaum, a producer at CBS's "60 Minutes," suggested that if you call him to pitch your "good" story, provide an anecdote or two that might illuminate the issue. It's one thing to pitch a story; it's quite another to find a way to bring it to life, supported by appealing visuals.

Newsweek's technology reporter Steven Levy readily shared his game book on how to pitch him with a good story that might make it into the weekly magazine.

"It's not so much about some original pitch," he said. "Do your homework and know the publication and the reporter you are pitching, making damn sure that what you are representing is something that would logically be written by that reporter for that publication.

"I don't think it takes a rocket scientist to know what I think is a great story — a LexisNexis search will do the trick. You'd find that I like to talk about the way technology changes people's lives, that I'm interested in the personalities of people who create great and groundbreaking stuff (and how they did it, and how it works), and that when I write about companies I'm into the narrative of their struggles."

The most effective media relations technique, said Levy, is to identify the right reporter and pitch the kind of story they would write about. Simple as that.

"Nothing counts for more than relationship and knowledge," John Pletz of the Austin, Texas, *American-Statesman* told me. "Knowing the person to whom you're making the pitch and knowing the publication are the best tools. The best pitches I get are from people who know our publication, what we cover, who we cover and how we like to cover it. Don't overthink it. It's not rocket science.

> "Nothing counts for more than relationship and knowledge. Knowing the person to whom you're making the pitch and knowing the publication are the best tools. The best pitches I get are from people who know our publication, what we cover, who we cover and how we like to cover it. Don't overthink it. It's not rocket science." — John Pletz, reporter, Austin *American-Statesman*

"E-mail remains the major change [in media relations] of the past decade," Pletz said. "It altered the dynamics of the relationship: No longer do you have to play endless rounds of phone tag to get your pitch across. More often than not, the e-mail will get through. The same can't be said of your phone call.

"Once you've succeeded in selling the story, e-mail becomes crucial in quickly dealing with follow-up issues, as well as distributing art (and photos), two more things that help get the story from pitch to publication."

Not long ago, a fax might have been a fairly good way to get a reporter's attention. Public relations agencies would *blast fax* hundreds of news releases to newsroom fax machines. But those days are over, for the most part. Blast fax gave way to blast e-mails that clog reporters' e-mail inboxes and are considered as annoying as e-mail spam. What journalists prefer is a more focused and targeted pitch on a story. By the way I found that many newsroom fax machines ran out of paper months ago, and no one bothered to refill them as a way to avoid the glut of faxed news releases.

"For our newsroom, short e-mails work best," Lisa Mullins told me. She's anchor and senior producer of "The World," a weekday international news program produced by the BBC that airs on public radio stations.

"Right now, there's a stack of pitches that have come over our fax machine in the last few days. About 5 percent will get looked at. Maybe faxes work well in some newsrooms. Not in ours. So it's best to find out the preferred, most efficient method of making your pitch.

"I don't expect public relations people to know precisely how a journalist works, but the more they know, the better," Mullins counseled.

Lisa Guernsey, who contributes to *The New York Times*, said that the best PR people have already done their homework before calling her, and they know what she is looking for in a story.

"They seem to know what might interest me, they are creative about offering story ideas, they understand that I write about trends more than companies, and they are willing to let an idea drop if I show no interest," Guernsey said.

On the other hand, Guernsey said, a PR person is wasting her time about a story that has recently appeared in the *Times* or is nowhere near her field of interest. That's an annoyance, she said.

"Sometimes," said NPR's Scott Simon, "people will hear you do one interview with a mushroom farmer and assume, somehow, that you have become a program for mushroom farmers. We will be flooded with pitches to interview mushroom farmers who are more witty, thoughtful or interesting than the one we have already had on.

"PR people should know: Because we do a mushroom farmer one week, we will probably not want to do another for some time to come."

> "PR people should know: Because we do a mushroom farmer one week, we will probably not want to do another for some

time to come." — Scott Simon, correspondent, National Public Radio

Jim Bohannon, talk-show host on Mutual and Westwood One Radio Networks, counsels media relations people to be selective in what they pitch and to whom and to be clear in explaining why his audience should care about it.

"I've been badgered by a few PR people with follow-up calls even though I said no. I know some clients are really important, and you can get desperate. But we won't forget who clung to our ankles," Bohannon said.

Dody Tsiantar, senior business reporter at *TIME* magazine in New York, is no stranger to giving public relations people insider perspective on how best to work with the news media. Here are some of her best tips.

"A few years back," she told me, "I spoke at a public relations convention here. I said this then, and I think it's the most valuable piece of advice a reporter can relay to someone in public relations:

"Do your homework. Sounds obvious, but so many people in the business don't do it. They'll cold call a reporter to pitch something that is totally irrelevant to that publication. From this side of the phone, it's really irritating — you want to bark back, 'Have you read this magazine? Would we really do this story? Have you ever seen anything like this in the magazine?'

"That said, the pitches that work are ones that show that the PR person has given the pitch some thought. They've explained what the story is about, why it's newsy and why we should cover it or write about it. What doesn't work is sending a generic letter or e-mail that shows little thought beyond typing in my name from a mailing list.

"I just thought of an example of a pitch that didn't work. Some new store sent a slew of chocolate covered candied apples to people in the building. The rules here require that if it's food or flowers then we need to go down to fetch the package ourselves. So, I got a call — and mind you it was on a Friday, our deadline day — to go down and pick up my package.

"It was nicely packaged in a plastic carton and a colorful clear orange plastic bag. I saw that it wasn't relevant, and I gave it to the woman manning the desk. Now this makes me think, what a waste. I really wish these companies would think about what they were doing. They think they have a mind-grabbing, brilliant idea and so often it falls completely flat.

"Another pet peeve of mine: I really get unnerved and irritated when someone sends a pitch via e-mail and then 30 minutes later calls me to tell me they sent me an e-mail. If I — or any reporter — is interested, we will follow up. Sometimes, to be fair, the call serves as a reminder — but I only appreciate it when it's a few days later. Then I remember that that e-mail interested me but I didn't follow up. But that quick follow up only serves to irritate the receiver of that call.

"One more follow-up to Do Your Homework: For really effective pitches, figure out what kind of deadline the people you're calling are dealing with. A pitch that arrives via e-mail on a busy Friday for me is likely to get buried — a call may result in a curt reply.

> "Do Your Homework: For really effective pitches, figure out what kind of deadline the people you're calling are dealing with. A pitch that arrives via e-mail on a busy Friday for me is likely to get buried — a call may result in a curt reply." — Dody Tsiantar, senior business reporter, *TIME*

"Don't leave voicemail messages either, asking someone to call without explaining what it is. In fact, don't leave any at all — follow up a day or so later with another e-mail. As the department head of the business and bonus business sections here, I get dozens of calls and dozens of e-mails every day — in one week I get around 500 — that it simply gets too overwhelming to return them. To stand out, a PR rep needs to be thoughtful and considerate in their approach — and the best way to do that is to DO YOUR HOMEWORK." Tsiantar added the capital letters for emphasis.

I spoke with and exchanged e-mails with dozens of journalists for this book, but Dody Tsiantar of *TIME* is among the most open about helping media relations people better communicate with the media. She makes her living writing interesting stories and can tell in an instant what's good and what's fluff.

However, Paul Andrews, technology reporter for *The Seattle Times*, has a slightly sardonic perspective after nearly 40 years as a journalist working with PR people. He thinks they have bad timing and seemingly work in a fog, caught up in a repetitive nature and forever oblivious to the needs of reporters.

"I see PR people as caught in a perpetual Hobson's choice," he said. "When the media needs them most, they are least available and willing to help. When the media has no need for them, the make their presence most felt."

"Hobson's choice" apparently originated with the behavior of a 16th-century stable manager in Cambridge, England — Thomas Hobson — who required every customer to take either the horse nearest the stable door or none at all, to keep popular horses from being overworked.

A CNN producer reminds us that journalists will remember who is good at media relations and who isn't. Certainly Paul Andrews is one of those who will remember.

Sandra Pinkard, who produces "The Diane Rehm Show" on National Public Radio, says "Most PR people I hear from are quick, to the point and respectful of my time. I also really appreciate the help I get from some in-house public relations people during off-hours, such as over weekends."

A reporter at *The Miami Herald* suggested, "Be candid with reporters when pitching a story idea; don't oversell or hype a story because it just hurts your credibility. Too often I have found PR people pitching their best-case scenario version, or the angle they want written, but that version falls apart once the reporting starts. And that puts a cloud over the whole thing.

"If you don't know, or won't really be able to give access, lay it out. There's nothing worse than starting to report something along certain contours offered by a public relations professional then realizing that the pitch was wrong, or manipulative or just plain ignorant."

> "If you don't know, or won't really be able to give access, lay it out. There's nothing worse than starting to report something along certain contours offered by a public relations professional then realizing that the pitch was wrong, or manipulative or just plain ignorant." — Reporter, *Miami Herald*

When pitching a story to a television news program, remember that there are big differences in style between network and local news. Television news is all about visuals, visuals, visuals.

A producer for the ABC's "World News Tonight" pointed out that most public relations people "do not have a solid understanding of what kind of stories producers at national networks — versus local stations — can get on their programs. Many PR people also seem unprepared to answer basic questions about visuals involved in their pitch — obviously an essential piece of any story for television."

She went on to say that "it can be frustrating when PR people only seem to know the two- or three-sentence 'headline' of a story but cannot answer more in-depth questions that come up in initial conversations. We producers love getting good story ideas and are more open to pitch them to our superiors if we, ourselves, can get a solid and quick handle on what the story is all about."

Nora Dennehy, a television producer at BBC News in London, said public relations people "need to have a peg for a particular story and then need to be able to supply or point us in the direction of good case studies or experts for their particular story and for television they need to understand that we always must have pictures to illustrate a particular point."

Timing can be everything in landing good media coverage of your story. Broadcast producer and journalist Pat Piper said, "Anticipate. Know when a congressional committee is going to schedule a hearing, and get out there ahead of it. Know when an anniversary of some sort is coming, and get out in front of it."

Another piece of advice: Don't play favorites. Washington, D.C., newspaperman Lyle Denniston said, "Nothing so infuriates a journalist working for a respectable news organization as to discover that a PR organization is serving media organizations differently, giving special favor and attention to a few. You will recognize this as the resentment of PR catering to Bigfoot news organizations.

"I am always baffled, in fact, to discover that a PR organization intent on reaching a wide segment of the public is willing to treat some news organization's readers or listeners as if they were second-class, simply because they are getting news from someone other than a Bigfoot. Medium or small news outlets do not need flattery, but neither do they need to be ignored."

And be realistic. Pat Piper tells of his worst experience with a media relations person, while producing "The Larry King Show": "A PR lady called to say she had a Russian TV anchorwoman — the Russian version of Paula Zahn. I said 'yes' to an interview. The anchor lady shows up at the studio and can't speak English." The public relations person never mentioned that little detail.

The best people in media relations, according to Richard Serrano of the *Los Angeles Times*, "are those who are honest and forthright with information, willing to steer you to the right aspect of a story without compromising their side. The worst are those who refuse to comment or cooperate and end up actually hurting their client or organization."

Lisa Guernsey of *The New York Times* sums it up by saying, "Public relations people can be extremely helpful, and the ones who impress me most are those who admit their limitations up front."

Effective media relations today is built on a foundation of respect, trust and a working relationship with reporters who have an interest in your organization and your story. It requires staying disciplined, a learning of what the media needs for a news story, keeping up to date on what specific reporters are writing and adding a healthy dose of good timing.

Before you even pick up the phone, make sure you have done your homework. Match the story of your media pitch with the right journalist. Be concise in what you say. Explain the potential importance or relevance of your story idea to the reporter's audience. If there are several sides to the story, build your own credibility and that of your organization by providing a brief but comprehensive perspective, including the other side's point of view. Offer background details, facts and statistics. Suggest how the story might be supported by visuals or photos. Most of all, get to the point, and don't be long-winded.

By being attuned to how media relations works from a journalist's perspective, an organization can enjoy accurate news coverage that is credible and influential toward achieving whatever goals it has established or can imagine.

Facing the Wolf Pack

Much of this book has focused on media relations from a journalist's perspective — understanding how journalists approach their jobs and what elements need to come together to create legitimate news. This understanding of the news media can give you a competitive edge and prepare you to speak with the media.

An interview with the news media can occur at any time and any place. An interview can be planned or occur spontaneously, without warning. An interview may result because you have called a contact at the local newspaper with a good, timely story about your organization — or because the telephone rings and a reporter at the other end of the line is asking for just a few minutes of your time to answer some questions.

Either way the primary objective of effective media relations is to communicate the story you want to tell as clearly and accurately as possible in a controlled way that will help ensure that good publicity for you or your organization.

The job of a reporter is to ferret out a story that will be of interest to readers, listeners or viewers.

An interview is not a conversation. It is a ritual in which the reporter seeks a news story, sometimes based on a preconceived notion, and you want to deliver focused messages that credibly tell your story. You want good coverage; the reporter wants news. Remember, it's not a conversation.

One of the most important rules is to avoid being interviewed when you are tired or angry. During Hurricane Katrina in 2005, we saw an exhausted and often angry Mayor C. Ray Nagin saying to reporters that 10,000 people had died in New Orleans. He didn't know how many people had died, and we all knew he was guessing. He was wrong.

Sure, he had every right to be angry at the incompetence and lack of timely response by the federal government, and many of us sympathized but it didn't help Nagin's credibility when he vented his fury, using profanity, on radio rather than in phone calls to Washington. As mayor of a major city who had been thrust into the world media spotlight, he had the responsibility to communicate accurate news, not guesses or anger, and he fumbled.

It's also important to know when to stop talking, especially about issues outside of your area of expertise. It's important to know when to shut up.

Cindy Sheehan, the brokenhearted mother who lost her son Casey to the Iraq war in 2004, had the world on her side when she camped outside President George W. Bush's ranch in Texas, seeking to meet with the president. The more Bush ignored her, the more sympathetic media coverage she got, until she started answering questions about Israel and Palestine, a completely irrelevant subject about which she knew nothing.

The lesson is to limit your area of expertise, and remember Grover Cleveland who said, "I never got in trouble with things I didn't say." At least it's a quote often attributed to that president.

> "I never got in trouble with things I didn't say." — Grover Cleveland, president of the United States, 1885 to1889 and 1893 to1897

At that point, conservative bloggers — many of the same people who attacked presidential hopeful John Kerry in 2004 — quickly went on the attack against Sheehan with a deluge of quotable quotes for the media and a smear campaign, including a claim that she was disgracing her dead son's legacy "by serving as a pawn for well-organized, anti-American activist groups." Bloggers said Sheehan "is a willing poster child for radical left-wing America haters ... is using her son's death ...

is cruelly robbing our fallen soldiers of the high honor that they deserve."

If you are not convinced yet of the power of blogs to influence the media, all you need to do is Google what happened to Kerry and Shee-han as a result of these vicious attacks by mostly invisible bloggers who got the media's attention, primarily because someone knew how to craft a quotable quote — the sort of clever, short phrase that reporters love for their stories.

Blogs and other emerging technology are being used as positive and constructive tools of media relations, as I have discussed earlier in this book.

Here's a list of interview dos and don'ts that I have observed from many years as a network news correspondent and then as a strategic communications agency executive.

First, the things you can do in an interview:

Always remember, it's your agenda. You do an interview not to help out a reporter but to communicate a positive message or image about your organization. Set your own boundaries. If a reporter calls out of the blue for an interview, you are under no obligation to drop every-thing and give an interview at that moment. Explain that you are fin-ishing up something and will call the reporter back in 30 minutes. Ask about the subject he or she wants to discuss. Never ask for a list of spe-cific questions, because this compromises the working ethics of jour-nalism, and you will start off on the wrong foot. Then take that 30 minutes or so to focus on what you want to say and communicate in the interview. This time will also help settle nerves that many people experience when contacted by the news media.

Always think three. Think of three messages you want to communi-cate in the interview. Think of how to deliver each message in an inter-esting and concise way. This is the core of what you want to communicate in the interview, so be prepared to stick with these mes-sages. Memorize them. By having three messages you can enhance control of an interview by providing depth and perspective. One message is emotional in nature, such as a shared human experience. One message is logical; "it only makes sense." And one message is analytical, backing up your other messages with facts and data. These three messages — emotional, logical and analytical — work together to present your side in the most compelling and controllable manner possible. This tactic boosts your chances of controlling the interview and landing a good story.

Always seek opportunities to bridge to your three points. A *bridge* is an interview tactic to control and redirect an interview back to the subject that you want to talk about. If the reporter asks a question, for example, that is far afield from what you want to talk about, no problem. Acknowledge the reporter by answering the question briefly, then bridge back to your messages. A bridge can be just a few words, such as "I believe one of the most important things to remember is ..." or "We need to keep in mind that ..." And then get back on track with your messages. Remember, it's your interview so make the most of it.

I recall once, as a young reporter in Washington, D.C., watching Sen. Edward Kennedy being interviewed by a gaggle of reporters in a hallway of the United States Capitol building. I remember being in awe of the poise and skills that allowed him, despite having questions thrown at him from all directions, to stay focused on precisely what he wanted to say. I imagined that if I were to say something like, "Excuse me, Senator, your fly is open!" he would not even look down but would instinctively use a bridge phrase like "Yes, I know," and transition immediately back to his message. Of course I didn't really say anything like that ... but I was tempted.

Always anticipate all questions. When you know in advance that a reporter is doing an interview, you can do a little online research on other stories the reporter has written and can get a good feel for what questions will be asked. Never go into an interview without first making a list of questions, even tough questions, you believe a reporter might ask. Ask colleagues to join in this exercise. It's a good way to quickly rehearse what you might say in an interview. If you wing it, you are headed for trouble and may lose any chance for control of the interview and the outcome you desire.

Always know when to stop. The best answer to a reporter's question is a concise answer. The shorter the answer, the better. I cannot tell you the hundreds of times I have heard a reporter ask a question that deserves just a 30-second response but receives a five-minute answer that makes the reporter's eyes glaze over. It's like asking someone what time it is, and then the person builds you a clock. As a general rule, keep answers to 30 seconds or less during a broadcast interview and to a minute or less in an interview with the print media. If a reporter thinks a certain answer is too short, he or she can always ask a follow-up question.

Always answer the question you were asked. Listen to each question. Answer that question. Interviews are stressful enough without your attempting to interpret or analyze what you think the reporter's motives might be. If you don't like the direction of a question, answer it briefly and bridge back to your own talking points.

Always try to use quotable quotes. Use colloquialisms, quote someone famous or use a memorable play on words, if appropriate, to make your point. Reporters love quotable quotes. Such quotes can make you look good in an interview and control the direction of the story.

Always back up message points with statistics and facts. When you use credible data to make your point in an interview, you earn respect and credibility.

Always remember that how you say it is as important as what you say. In an interview, be genuine and sincere. Take some time before an interview to — as they say — get yourself in a good place. Go into an interview with a positive frame of mind. Don't be afraid to smile. Use your voice, eyes and expressions to show passion in your words.

Always maintain eye contact. Whether in a newspaper or television interview, look at the reporter, and never allow your eyes to stray. Don't sneak a glance at the camera lens or someone standing nearby.

Eye contact tells a reporter that this interview is the most important thing you are doing right now. If your eyes wander during a television interview, the perception may be that you are nervous.

Always remember that a microphone is always on. Never say anything silly or inappropriate, assuming a microphone has been switched off. It can happen to anyone. Back in the 1980s then-president Ronald Reagan, an old pro with the media, who should have known better, jokingly said, "We start bombing Russia in five minutes." A microphone was on, and Reagan's playful remark made embarrassing headlines around the world.

Always briefly summarize your key points at the end of the interview. You have the forum — the spotlight — so make the most of it. A summary provides you with a final opportunity to deliver your three messages, again.

Now, for a short list of things to avoid when doing in an interview:

Never talk off the record. It kills your credibility with the news media.

Never say anything you don't want to see in print or on the air. If you are angry with someone or a situation, don't use the interview as a forum to say something casually on the side that you don't think a reporter will hear or use. An interview is not a time to kid around.

Never take it personally or get defensive. Reporters, in most cases, are just out doing their job of finding news stories. Work with them, and everyone wins. The days of ambush journalism ended years ago.

Never assume an interview is a conversation. There is nothing casual or chatty about an interview, no matter how informal a particular reporter's style might be. A reporter is always working to find a good story.

Never make up answers. If you don't know, say so and promise to get the information and respond promptly.

So often when someone claims he or she has been misquoted in an interview, it's because of something the interviewee said. An apparent misquote usually happens because the person being interviewed has said something contradictory or ambiguous, even though the journalist usually and wrongfully gets the blame. It happens often because the interviewee simply talked too much.

The same guidelines apply for doing television or radio interviews, except there are the added distractions of microphones, lights and cameras. No problem. Here is a simple crib sheet I've used for years with clients to help them control broadcast interviews and communicate clear and persuasive messages:

- Be accessible to reporters.

- Tell the truth.

- For TV and radio interviews, modulate your voice to avoid a monotone that sounds like Connie Conehead. Remember the Conehead family of "Saturday Night Live" fame?

- Be prepared. If you don't know the issue inside and out, find a colleague who does and have him do the interview. If the colleague turns out to be terrified of the microphone, have him thoroughly brief you, giving you more information than you need to get the organization's story and position across.

- When asked a question, get to the point quickly. This is perhaps the most important tip when doing a broadcast interview — *get to the point quickly.*

- Never use 27 words when four will do.

- If you are doing a television interview with other people, act as if the camera is always focused on you, whether or not you are speaking or being spoken to. Don't scratch your nose while the other guy is talking. Don't scratch your nose while you are talking.

- Look at the person who is speaking — not at the camera. When you talk, look at the person who addressed you — not at the camera. Don't stare off into space.

- If you're on a panel, really listen to what the other side is saying and look interested.

- Pretend the only person watching or listening is your grandmother.

As you might expect, how you look on television — your style of clothing, posture, expressions and hand gestures — is nearly as important as what you have to say. Your appearance helps to build credibility.

- Wear clothes that will not distract people from what you are saying, such as fairly conservative business attire in mostly solid colors. Incidentally men no longer need to wear blue shirts for TV interviews because of today's high-quality cameras. Yet the color of what you wear can work to send subtle and influential signals to an audience. For example when Vice President Dick Cheney gave his first television interview about the hunting accident in which he blasted Texas attorney Harry Whittington with birdshot from his shotgun, Cheney was dressed in a dark suit and pink tie. A red tie is part of Cheney's signature business attire, but in the environment of accepting responsibility for shooting someone, red would make too bold and authoritative a statement. Pink, on the other hand, is the color of innocence and warmth. Clearly the vice president's pink tie worked to his favor.

- If being interviewed while standing, stand up straight. Slouching can send a message of being bored or having a negative attitude.

- If giving an interview while seated, sit up straight. If at a table, lean in slightly to show that you are engaged in providing honest answers. People who slouch back in their chairs during interviews can send a signal, right or wrong, of arrogance.

- It's helpful to learn something about TV makeup in case the guys interviewing you don't have someone there to powder your nose or create cheekbones.

- Avoid waving your hands around during a television interview. It's distracting and might make you appear like someone in a used-car commercial or one of today's crop of overly dramatic TV reporters. If you want to make a point with a hand gesture, do so with one hand and conservative, slow movements.

- Look natural and friendly, but don't smile at the interviewer while you're talking about something serious.

Newsmakers I have coached have been guided by these simple rules when facing cameras and microphones, often during impromptu and high-pressure situations. The ability to master the protocol of broadcast interviews has allowed them to focus on their words and messages they want to deliver. As a result, that credibility has helped build many enduring relationships with journalists.

Lastly, if you are ambushed by a surprise question, heed the advice of former Secretary of Defense Robert S. McNamara: Just answer the question you *wish* had been asked.

People who have mastered the discipline of being interviewed and talking with journalists on a high level of mutual respect and trust, know the effectiveness of using the news media as an enormously powerful and influential communication tool to reach vast and important audiences. Those people are today's leaders.

The Best Marketing Weapon

Media relations is all about communicating effectively to vast audiences through the news media.

An organization can't build such credibility by purchasing a display advertisement on the front page of a major daily newspaper in America. That newspaper real estate isn't for sale. Yet it is possible, through good media relations, for that organization to get a favorable news story on the front page, complete with the implied third-party credibility that comes from having a newspaper report good things about the organization. Effective media relations is the most powerful weapon in an organization's marketing arsenal.

Over the years I have witnessed political greatness defined, such as the image of Ronald Reagan, through media relations, guided by people of intellect and media smarts, like my friend Michael Deaver.

Deaver's public relations firm in Washington, D.C., for example, created a media blitz that helped to send the report by the National Commission on Terrorist Attacks Upon the United States, the Sept. 11 commission, rocketing to the top of national bestseller lists, which resulted in a nomination for a National Book Award. The media campaign influenced Congress, the administration and key liberal and conservative influencers to embrace the commission's findings upon release.

The blanket of media coverage they generated reached across the country and around the world. The commission's Web site received more than 50 million hits in the first 24 hours as a result of the coverage. Throughout the coverage, the message the Commission wanted to deliver to America was clear.

You see, more often than not, such a high level of media coverage doesn't just happen by accident; *it is made to happen* by skilled media relations pros with extensive contacts among journalists.

My own work in media relations has centered on enhancing the competitive positioning, brand image and reputations of corporations. Many times I have worked with clients to devise ways to sell products or persuasive messages through the powerful clout of the news media.

One of my most memorable experiences happened when London Records asked me to find a way to propel sales of compact discs for the first Three Tenors Concert, which was about to happen in July of that year. London Records saw it as another opera recording, and that was a real challenge — opera recordings are not hot-selling items in America.

The company's top executives had set a seemingly unattainable sales goal of 200,000 CDs during the first two months of the recording's release. It appeared to be an impossible task, since the previously biggest selling opera recording in America had sold just 50,000 CDs over three years.

So off I flew to Rome to attend the concert and look for a story angle to pitch to the news media that would make news and publicize the recording in order to stimulate sales.

As I sat in the audience beside the legendary coloratura soprano Beverly Sills, watching the amazing performance by Luciano Pavarotti, José Carreras and Plácido Domingo, on a stage in the ancient Baths of Caracalla along the Appian Way in Rome, the idea struck me. This was not an opera performance as much as it was a *historic event*, a never before happening. And that made all the difference in the world in positioning it before the news media to be successful.

The royalty, celebrities and social elite of Europe had come together not for an opera concert but because they recognized history in the making. Pavarotti, Carreras and Domingo, all revered stars, had never before performed together on the same stage, and it was making headlines around the world, except in the United States.

Once back home, I made quiet soundings among friends and contacts in the national news media to find someone who might be interested in the story. The initial reaction was as if *opera* were a five-letter dirty word. No one had heard of the concert, and no one really cared ... no one except Cindy Carpien, the much-adored producer of National Public Radio's "Weekend Edition" with Scott Simon on Saturday.

Cindy was intrigued by the fact that she hadn't heard of such a big event. There had not been one mention of it in the U.S. news media. Over a period of about a week, we talked several times to figure out how the story could be told on radio. It didn't seem feasible to interview only one of the tenors without the others, but to get all three together for such an interview would be impossible. So I proposed an interview with someone who had worked individually with each of the three tenors for 20 years and finally had the chance to work with all three together — English recording engineer James Locke. Cindy agreed.

Locke was a colorful interview. As excerpts from the first Three Tenors recording were played on NPR, he described the "magic" that filled the air that evening in Rome.

He painted a verbal picture for the radio audience that allowed listeners to experience what that evening of music must have been like amid the setting at the 3rd-century Baths of Caracalla and the historic pines of Rome. His vivid descriptions took listeners there and provided a behind-the-scenes glimpse of the event and who attended. Not once did he mention the word *opera*, but instead he described why the *historic event* had brought thousands of people together in Rome.

The piece ran 12 minutes on a Saturday morning and was heard on nearly 400 NPR stations by an audience in the millions, primarily baby boomers — a generation that enjoys an appealing new trend.

Within a week all 200,000 CDs of the first Three Tenors Concert recording were sold. It was the power of one cleverly developed story angle on a radio news program that was heard by the right audience. The recording went on to be the biggest-selling classical CD in history.

I wrote no news releases, no fact sheets, no media kits. The story happened by making phone calls to established contacts in the news media and working with them to develop an angle and provide someone to interview. As we've said elsewhere in this book, it's all about relationships and understanding how the media works.

Balanced and accurate news media coverage of a business or organization creates lasting goodwill, boosts an image, sells products and enhances credible influence more effectively than any other kind of mass communication. It will help to build a brand with enduring credibility.

Good media relations will help an organization break out of competitive clutter. It really doesn't matter whether you are the largest or No. 1. If the media likes you and is captivated by what you say, then you are perceived as a leader.

News in today's world is reported literally every minute, around the clock, via the traditional channels of newspapers, wire services, magazines, television and radio — but also through Web sites and an ever-increasing variety of online sources, including blogs and podcasts.

But despite the diversity of today's types of media, media relations comes down to getting to know journalists and what they need to do their jobs, understanding what is news and what isn't, and working together with reporters on a professional level to provide the background information, facts and interviews they need to make a story happen.

And all along the way, those charged with media relations must be able to express enthusiasm without sounding like publicists. Clear and credible messages in everyday words must be crafted and neatly tucked inside the context of legitimate news. Clever and contemporary media relations techniques, consistently and professionally managed, will deliver impressive results and make news. Great news media coverage can be the stuff of legends.

978-1-58348-468-5
1-58348-468-X

Made in the USA
Lexington, KY
12 February 2013